The Commercial Litigator's Job

A Survival Guide

Cristen Sikes Rose

Series created and edited by International Legal Publishers, LLC

GP|Solo

ABA General Practice, Solo & Small Firm Division

Cover design by ABA Publishing.

The materials contained herein represent the opinions and views of the authors and/or the editors, and should not be construed to be the views or opinions of the law firms or companies with whom such persons are in partnership with, associated with, or employed by, nor of the American Bar Association or the General Practice, Solo and Small Firm Section, unless adopted pursuant to the bylaws of the Association.

Nothing contained in this book is to be considered as the rendering of legal advice, either generally or in connection with any specific issue or case; nor do these materials purport to explain or interpret any specific bond or policy, or any provisions thereof, issued by any particular franchise company, or to render franchise or other professional advice. Readers are responsible for obtaining advice from their own lawyers or other professionals. This book and any forms and agreements herein are intended for educational and informational purposes only.

Printed in the United States of America

09 08 07 06 05 5 4 3 2 1

Library of Congress Cataloging-in-Publication Data

Rose, Cristen Sikes, 1973-
   The commercial litigator's job : a survival guide / by Cristen Sikes Rose.
      p. cm.
   Includes index.
   ISBN 1-59031-555-3
      1. Business law—United States—Trial practice. 2. Trial practice—United States. I. Title.

KF8925.C55R67 2005
346.7307—dc22

                                                                        2005026811

Discounts are available for books ordered in bulk. Special consideration is given to state bars, CLE programs, and other bar-related organizations. Inquire at Book Publishing, ABA Publishing, American Bar Association, 321 North Clark Street, Chicago, Illinois 60610-4714.

www.ababooks.org

"Never assume, lieutenant. The world is full of dead men who lived by assumption."

— Unknown army officer

Contents

Foreword

This guide is for new litigators. It gives junior associates basic instruction on the assignments that they are likely to receive in the commercial litigation departments of most law firms. This guide is not intended to be a summary of the law. It is more like a recipe book for turning out legal work that satisfies the palates of the senior lawyers who give you your work and write your reviews.

You also need this book because law school did not teach you things like why you should not rely on being able to use an electronic calendar in court (some courts do not permit them past security) or how to handle inadvertent disclosure of privileged material.

If not already aware, you soon will learn that few lawyers are gifted managers. The partners and senior associates who assign your work are not always around or available to teach you the basics. But they still expect you to know them and if you do not, your review, reputation, and career may suffer.

The good news is that as a junior associate you can make yourself look good by making the senior lawyers look good in front of the client and the court. At the same time, the consequence of your minor mistakes may be multiplied because, in addition to harming your own reputation, your mistake may hurt the credibility of the lawyers to whom you report.

Cautionary Note

Courts may not accept pleadings that fail to comply with all applicable rules. One court, for example, requires that any motion filed include mailing labels for all counsel on the case and will reject the motion if you forget to include the mailing labels. If a court rejects your answer to a complaint and there is no time to correct it, your client will be in default. This is not a career-enhancing experience. So read on.

The procedures, advice, and forms contained in this book are based on the Federal Rules of Civil Procedure. Although the procedural rules of many state court systems are based on the Federal Rules, each court system has its own rules. Accordingly, and I cannot emphasize this strongly enough, it is imperative that you always consult the rules of the particular court system in which you are litigating. Individual courts within each court system may also have separate rules. Similarly, some judges have standing orders that govern procedures in their courtrooms. Courts' rules and judges' standing orders often are available on the courts' web sites and from each clerk's office.

About the Author

Cristen Sikes Rose graduated cum laude from Georgetown University in 1996 and was elected to the Order of the Coif upon her graduation from the College of William and Mary School of Law in 1999. In 1999, she started as an associate in the commercial litigation group of DLA Piper Rudnick Gray Cary US LLP's Washington, D.C. office, where she remains today. Ms. Rose's areas of practice include securities, corporate, commercial, and environmental litigation, and she has tried cases in state and federal courts and in private arbitrations. She also has drafted motions and briefs that have been filed in United States District Courts, in Courts of Appeal, and in the Supreme Court. Ms. Rose also regularly counsels clients on litigation risks and litigation avoidance. She serves as a mentor to junior associates at DLA Piper, and as a member of the firm's hiring committee and, in 2003, was the recipient of a firm-wide award recognizing her commitment to pro bono work.

CHAPTER 1

Surviving as a New Associate

Diligence and conscientious behavior have more to do with success as a junior associate than being intelligent or articulate.

Junior associates serve two principal roles: information gatherers and task accomplishers of the scores of small responsibilities that comprise a larger client matter.

As an information gatherer, a junior associate is closest to the discovery material upon which legal arguments are based and is most likely to know what documents and motions should be delivered or made. As a task accomplisher, a junior associate takes responsibility for personally performing a set of assigned tasks, so saying "I asked someone else to do it" is not a career-enhancing statement.

On the other hand, while junior associates are expected to work long hours and produce lots of work, they are not expected to have all of the answers.

But even at the most junior level, a new attorney will be responsible for leading a small team, including his or her secretary, a paralegal, and document processing staff. Successfully working with these professionals is important, and earning a reputation as someone who is difficult to work with will hurt you. You will miss the opportunity to learn from the staff, if not about the substance of your work, then at least about firm politics.

A few basic ingredients of good teamwork are these:

1. Learn everyone's name;

2. Delegate only those tasks that you have performed yourself at least once;

3. Be specific with both praise and criticism; and

4. Listen to and consider suggestions from the staff—they have worked at the firm longer than you have.

SHOULD YOU ACCEPT A NEW ASSIGNMENT AT ALL?

The instinctive reaction of most junior associates is to accept any assignment that comes along. Do not do this. Be very careful about taking more work than you can handle. "I was overworked" is not a valid excuse for delivering sloppy work to clients or senior lawyers. If you are too busy to do a good job, senior lawyers usually understand. They may not like it, but eventually they understand.

You must learn when you are too busy to take on a new project. This requires judgment, but the questions to ask yourself when considering new work are:

1.   Can I do a good job with everything I've already agreed to do? and

2.   Am I doing as much as I am capable of doing?

Always ask the person proposing a new project for the deadline. Then think about existing projects. Do their deadlines conflict with that of the new project? Do any of your existing projects involve travel or offsite work that would interfere with the new one? Does the new project interfere with existing ones in this way?

Where two (or more) attorneys assign work to you and a potential new assignment interferes with a preexisting one, you have two choices: (1) you can ask the first attorney to explain to the other attorney(s) that you are busy with her project and cannot accept a new assignment, or (2) you can send an e-mail to both attorneys explaining that you are happy to take the second assignment but cannot do so unless the deadline for the first assignment is flexible.

You are hard-working but not super-human. You are expected to do a good job on the work you agree to perform.

THINGS LAW SCHOOL WILL NEVER TEACH YOU

▶   Any document you hand a supervising lawyer should represent your best work. Never say "it's just a draft," even if the supervisor only asks for a draft.

▶   Find out if your firm is strict about Blue Book conventions. If so, you had better finally learn them.

▶   Anticipate, anticipate, anticipate! Always try to predict what the senior lawyers will want next and ask if you should do it.

► Do not blame others for your mistakes. In particular, never blame your secretary for anything. It is your responsibility to manage her and to review her work before it goes to someone else.

► Know where everything is filed. If your secretary has a well-established filing system, make sure you understand it.

► Never go into a supervisor's office without a pad and pen.

► When you are assigned to a new case, offer to assemble a working group list of each member of the team (including staff), with all home, office, and mobile contact information (including street addresses). Circulate a copy of the list to everyone named on it. The first time you send it around, ask everyone to look over their own listing to see if any corrections are necessary.

► Unless there is a special reason not to, always copy everyone on the working group list with all documents and information related to the case.

► Master the infrastructure:

 ▼ Fax machine (with billing codes).

 ▼ Telephone (with billing codes).

 ▼ Document vendors: photocopy center, imaging services, etc.

 ▼ Support staff (secretaries, paralegals, mailroom workers, couriers, library personnel, etc.). Get to know them—they can help you a lot.

SECTION 2

Organizational Advice

SUGGESTED DAILY ROUTINE

One of the most important things to manage as a young lawyer is deadlines. Clients and senior attorneys schedule their own work based upon the promised delivery of supporting work from junior lawyers. Consider the following:

(1) Do not arrive at your desk later than those to whom you report arrive at theirs.

(2) Check phone and e-mail messages; add them to "to do" lists.

- ▼ Keep "to do" lists for both general responsibilities and specific projects.

- ▼ Do not allow "to do" items, phone messages, or e-mails to accumulate.

(3) Review your calendar daily for upcoming deadlines and appointments.

(4) Review mail in your "In" box.

(5) Review open items on "to do" list. Decide which items need attention before noon, which need attention by the end of the day, and which can wait until the following day.

(6) Check advance sheets and/or legal newspapers to see if there is new law affecting any of the cases on which you are working.

(7) Begin billable work within thirty minutes of arriving. This sounds easy but is not. Doing so will help you focus on billable work early in the day, which, in turn, will keep you from staying late unnecessarily and will enhance your reputation for productivity.

(8) At the end of the day, make certain that all billable time has been recorded.

(9) Do not leave the office until phone messages and e-mails have been reviewed and handled appropriately.

ADVICE ON BILLING HOURS

Clients and senior lawyers (some of whom you have not met and will not meet) will monitor and scrutinize your billable hours very closely. You should monitor and scrutinize them at least as closely.

(1) Read and comply with your firm's policies regarding billing, recording time, and time entry.

(2) Record your billable hours throughout each day. This may sound easy, but it is not. When you are working on multiple small matters, record them whenever you finish working for one client and start working for another.

(3) Always submit your timesheets on time and under your firm's guidelines.

(4) Use detailed time entries in the active voice. Write "Analyzed minutes of the board of directors and stockholder correspondence." Do not say "Attention to discovery."

  ▼ A good general rule is that more detail is always better. Say "Analyzed lease for 1600 First Avenue property; analyzed correspondence between lessor and landlord." Do not say "Attention to real estate matters."

  ▼ Remember that your time entries are transcribed onto the client's bill and that some lawyers view timesheets as the best form of advertising. Ideally, the client would read their bill and think "Wow! You did all of that?" If your time entry reads "7.5 hours—attention to discovery," you are unlikely to get this reaction.

  ▼ Always bill accurately. Do not "pad" your time or record less time than you actually worked on a matter. You may feel that it took you too long to write a letter, but it is the billing attorney's responsibility to adjust your time, not yours.

  ▼ Avoid round numbers. Most people do not really work "8.0 hours." A timesheet showing lots of round numbers looks padded; 7.8 hours looks more realistic.

(5) When accepting an assignment, always ask if there are any special billing procedures or sensitivities. For example, some clients require attorneys to bill in tenths of an hour, while others require billing in different increments. In addition, some clients will require that you use special billing codes that they provide.

(6) Ask the assigning lawyer how many hours he estimates the project should take. If the expected time is more than ten hours or so, check with a supervising lawyer after four or five hours to determine if you are on the right track.

(7) Periodically assess how many total hours you have put into each project. Senior lawyers appreciate that you consider not just your own hours, but also the client's bill.

MANAGING A LITIGATION CALENDAR

Never miss a deadline. You or your firm may be the greatest advocates of the modern era, but if you are sloppy about deadlines, you will lose cases. Also, do not rely on a calendaring department, a paralegal, or a secretary to track your deadlines.

General Calendar Issues

▶ Your calendar is your most important professional tool. It can tell you when assignments are due, whether you can go on vacation, when you are due in court, whether tonight is a good night to go home early, and what you have been doing for the last few months. Pay attention to it.

▶ Train yourself to consult your calendar before making any time-consuming or time-sensitive commitment, whether personal or professional.

▶ You will have court-imposed deadlines as well as deadlines for delivery of material to supervisors and clients. Use your calendar for both. Do not forget to add deadlines for firm or client work to your calendar.

▶ Take care counting days. Always consult the applicable rules about how days are counted: Do you count all days or only business days? The answer may vary depending on how many days you are counting (e.g., if you are counting seven days or less, you may count business days only, but you will include calendar days if you are counting more than seven days). Are days added if particular methods of service are used (e.g., serving a document by mail may add three days)?

▶ Note what constitutes the end of the deadline day. Midnight? The close of the clerk's office at the courthouse (sometimes at 4:30 p.m.)? The close of business?

Electronic vs. Paper Calendars

You can track appointments and deadlines electronically or with a paper organizer.

THE ELECTRONIC METHOD

▶ The electronic method requires calendar software that has a "reminder" capability (such as Outlook) and an electronic organizer or PDA (a personal digital assistant, such as a Palm Pilot or Blackberry) that you can synchro-nize with your computer. The electronic method works as follows:

— Anytime you receive a pleading or discovery to which you must respond, check the court rules for the deadline and enter it on your computer.

— For major deadlines, such as the deadline for filing a motion for sum-mary judgment or the cut-off for discovery, set the reminder for thirty to forty-five days in advance. For tasks that take less time, such as responses to simple interrogatories, one to two weeks may be sufficient.

— When your "reminders" appear, notify those who assigned you the work of the impending deadlines. They will appreciate the notice.

▶ WARNING: Some courthouses do not permit electronic devices, including PDAs, in courtrooms. Accordingly, always take along a printout of your calendar for the next six to nine months when you go to court. That way, you will have your calendar if the judge wants to set a schedule. If the senior attorney on a case is not going to accompany you on a court date, you also may request that he provide you a printout of his schedule so that you will not create conflicts for him.

THE PAPER METHOD

▶ The paper method requires a paper desk calendar and a tickler system. The advantages of a paper calendar are that you can always have it with you, and you can easily see your deadlines.

▶ Calendars that permit you to view a month at a time and include space for notes on upcoming events are best. Enter deadlines on your calendar as they are set. Use the notes space to remind yourself of upcoming tasks and deadlines. Use the paper method as follows:

— Get an expandable file with slots numbered one through thirty-one (the days of the month).

— Copy deadline-related documents and put them in the numbered slot for the day of the month on which you want a reminder. Each morning, review the documents in that day's slot.

CHAPTER 3

Drafting Complaints

A complaint is often one of the first court documents a new associate is asked to draft. The importance of the complaint to a case cannot be overstated. It is the framework of the litigation.

TIPS AND SUGGESTIONS

1. *When litigation is filed or anticipated, notify the client of its obligation to preserve all evidence, regardless of its standard document retention policies.* As soon as a party knows that litigation is likely, it should begin preserving all relevant evidence. If the client has a policy of regularly destroying documents, that policy should be suspended. Jurisdictions and local rules vary regarding the consequences of destroying documents after litigation is likely (or has commenced), so check applicable law. In any case, ask your assigning attorney if the following steps are appropriate:

    ▼   Notify the client contact (usually a high-level employee such as the general counsel) of the obligation to preserve evidence.

    ▼   Send a memo to all company employees and others who may have relevant evidence (such as documents and e-mails), asking them to preserve it.

    ▼   Ask the company's information technology department to preserve any back-up tapes or the like and to suspend any functions that automatically delete documents and information (such as routine recycling of back-up tapes).

2. *Confirm the facts.* Before drafting a complaint, confirm that the facts to be pled in the complaint are accurate. Inaccuracies in the complaint harm the credibility of both the assigning attorney and the client before the court and create the risk of a Federal Rule 11 (or state rule) sanction and/or a malicious prosecution claim.

Take the following steps prior to filing the complaint:

▼ Gather and review all relevant documents.

▼ Interview your client and potential witnesses. Interviews tell you what people know and who else you should interview. Also, be aware that you may need to interview company witnesses separately from the general counsel. The presence of the general counsel during an interview may make the witness uneasy and less likely to tell you what really happened.

▼ Ask yourself whether all potential parties to the claim have the capacity to sue or be sued. For example, defunct entities generally do not have this capacity.

▼ Are there any arbitration clauses implicated by the potential claim(s)? Will your client be required to pursue its claims in arbitration, as opposed to court? If there is an arbitration clause, is arbitration good or bad for your client's claims? If it is bad, consider whether you can plead your claims creatively to avoid invoking the arbitration clause.

▼ Does the defendant have insurance that may cover the amount your client hopes to recover? Should your complaint be crafted to maximize the chance that the defendant's insurance policies will provide coverage? For example, many policies cover defendants for negligent acts but not intentional ones.

▼ Use the Internet to find information about the parties. Many government agencies have extensive records online that may include information about your adversary's problems with those agencies.

▶ Depending upon the resources of your firm and the advice of the assigning attorney, you may ask your firm's research librarian to make the first attempt at gathering this information as well as the remaining items in this list.

▼ Check the Securities and Exchange Commission's web site (www .sec.gov). If the company is publicly traded, the EDGAR database provides online copies of the detailed reports that public companies are required to file. Click "Search for Company Filings" under "Filings and Forms (EDGAR)." Look for forms 8-K, 10-Q, 10-K, 14A, and the series of "S" registration statements, among others.

▼ Check online commercial databases that contain business and asset locator tools such as Lexis and Westlaw. These provide addresses, property ownership data, corporate status, and information about a party's involvement in other litigation, among other things.

▼ Check the adversary's web site and print each page. Collect this as early as possible, because parties to litigation may change their web sites after a complaint has been filed.

▼ Run the parties' and witnesses' names through a search engine on the Internet such as Google™. These searches might provide you with a party's or a witness' educational or employment backgrounds, publications they authored, and news reports about them.

3. *Decide what claims to assert and what relief to request.* This may be more art than science. The assigning attorney should tell you what claims she thinks you should assert and what relief you should seek, but contribute your own suggestions and make sure that you suggest all additional causes of action that may be related and available. Also, advise the assigning attorney of any reasons against asserting certain claims, such as the existence of arbitration clauses and the availability of insurance (see above). Get copies of complaints previously drafted by or for the assigning lawyer: do they seem to assert as many claims as possible or only those for which immediate proof can be found?

4. *Note specific requirements of claims you make.* Are you required to plead a specific amount of damages? Are you required to plead any claims with specificity (such as fraud and claims involving an element of fraud)? Make sure to plead each element of each cause of action or count. Make sure sufficient facts are pled to support each element.

If your client has direct knowledge of a fact that must be pled, that fact may be pled directly: "Defendant did X." If your client lacks direct knowledge of a fact that must be pled but has indirect knowledge of the fact (e.g., from others or through reasonable inference), you may plead that fact based upon "information and belief": "Upon information and belief, Defendant did X." Information and belief allegations generally should be reserved for facts that are within the knowledge or control of another party. Some case law also suggests that you must plead the basis (i.e., the facts) on which the information and belief is based, particularly if "information and belief" allegations are pled in support of a fraud claim.

5. *Consider what relief to request.* The relief you are entitled to request often is a function of the causes of action you assert and statutory and case law decided thereunder. For example, statutes and cases may define the damages a plaintiff may seek for negligence claims or, in a breach of contract action, whether a plaintiff is entitled to seek rescission as opposed to the contradictory remedy of damages, or both. Again, you should seek input from the assigning attorney and/or the client on what relief to request, but you should also research the type of relief available

and make suggestions. In addition, after requesting specific relief in a complaint, it is standard practice to include a generic request for "any and all other relief to which the plaintiff is entitled."

▼ Do not forget to consider whether the plaintiff is entitled to recover punitive damages. Punitive damages are special damages intended to punish the defendant for its actions, which provide recovery to the plaintiff beyond what actual damages the plaintiff can prove to have suffered. Entitlement to punitive damages is a function of statutory and case law. If the claims you assert and the facts that support them provide a basis for recovery of punitive damages under the law, you should expressly seek them in the complaint.

6. *Know your audience.* All complaints should effectively convey your client's story, but never forget that, in most cases, you are drafting a public document with your client's and your firm's names on it. There are reporters who cover the courts who may read complaints as soon as they are filed. You should not write anything in a complaint that would make you or your client uncomfortable if it appeared in the morning newspaper. Some issues to consider (and discuss with your assigning attorney) regarding the complaint:

▼ Ask the assigning attorney for an example of a prior complaint that she liked. This example should tell you the tone preferred by the assigning lawyer. Does the favorite complaint read more like an instruction manual or a sermon?

▼ If sensitive business information or trade secrets must be pled in the complaint, consider whether you can file the complaint (or at least the exhibits, if any) under seal. Check case law in your jurisdiction for the standard for sealing court documents.

▼ Do not assume that a reader of the complaint will have any familiarity with the facts or with any party to the case. The court, for example, may be unfamiliar with the case, the parties, and the subject matter. Also, it may be helpful to include facts that make an implicit point for your client. For example, if you represent Johnny Appleseed in his suit against ABC Corp., the largest manufacturer of widgets in the world, you may want to create a contrast between the affluence of the defendant and the "poor little plaintiff."

▼ Do not include extraneous language or artificial formality; write short, clear sentences with the same formality you would use in normal business correspondence.

▼ Invective and melodrama are rarely effective in complaints. This language makes the allegations look exaggerated and less persuasive.

▼ Avoid legalisms, such as "heretofore," "said complainant," and the like. Legalisms sound pompous and forced.

▼ Avoid sarcasm and attempts at humor. They make the drafting attorney appear unprofessional and waste the court's time.

▼ Use good judgment in deciding how to reflect your client's view of the defendant. Your client may describe the defendants as "freeloading thieves," but this phrase does not belong in the complaint.

▼ Do not assume any subject-specific sophistication. For example, if the basis of the complaint is the failure of complicated technology to work as promised, explain in plain English the purpose and intended function of the failed technology before delving into the details of its failure.

▼ So what should your complaint say? It should assert, in a firm and professional manner, that the defendant violated your client's rights and/or the law and that your client was harmed as a result. It should also specify how your client was harmed.

7. *Broad vs. narrow: the strategic debate.* A key aspect of litigation strategy is the timing of the release of important facts to the opposing party. Discuss with the assigning attorney whether her strategy for the case supports "showing the cards" in the complaint or providing only what is absolutely required by the pleading rules. In your discussion with the assigning attorney, consider the following:

Detailed complaints. A complaint with more factual detail (i) provides the defendant with more facts against which he must defend, (ii) forces the defendant to question his own position more precisely than would a more general set of facts, and (iii) demonstrates that the plaintiff has committed thought, research, and resources to the case.

Reasons to use a detailed complaint are:

▼ The plaintiff's claims are of the type that often draw a Motion to Dismiss from the defendant and/or are subject to heightened pleading standards (such as fraud claims).

▼ The plaintiff seeks preliminary injunctive relief. Complaints seeking preliminary injunctions are usually heard by a judge within days after they are filed, so you must present the best possible case immediately.

▼ Some state laws and procedural rules adhere to the "four corners" doctrine, which limits admissible evidence to what is stated in the complaint and what can be judicially noticed. If you are filing the complaint in one of these states, you may want to include more detail to ensure that important evidence is not ruled inadmissible.

"Bare bones" complaints. A complaint with less factual detail gives the defendant less knowledge of the facts upon which the plaintiff's claims are based.

Reasons to file a complaint with minimal detail are:

▼ The amount of discovery a defendant may conduct depends, in part, on the contents of the complaint. A factually detailed complaint may invite the defendant to engage in broader discovery of your client.

▼ A detailed complaint reveals more about the plaintiff's case. For example, a complaint that pleads all facts relevant (rather than necessary) to a claim warns the defendant to investigate all areas described and to prepare their witnesses in those areas at their depositions.

8. *Determine what the client wants.* You should also consult with the assigning attorney and/or the client about what the client hopes to achieve by filing a complaint and what it hopes to avoid. Some issues to consider:

▼ Does the client plan to maintain a business relationship with the defendant? If so, the tone of the complaint should be especially careful and factual.

▼ Are there areas that the client does not want known to the public? For example, in a contract dispute, the contract is described in (and often attached to) the complaint. This makes the contract (or the dispute) available to competitors to use for competitive advantage.

9. *Determine whether you must file a verified complaint.* A verified complaint is one containing an oath that the facts alleged therein are true and accurate to the best of the knowledge, information, and belief of the person giving the oath. In this regard, verified complaints resemble, and may be treated as, affidavits. Use of verified complaints generally should be reserved for cases where one is required by rule or statute, such as ex parte requests for temporary injunctive relief and shareholder derivative actions. In all other cases, the use of verified complaints is rare and unnecessary.

10. *Follow the pleading rules.* Follow the pleading rules of the court in which you are filing the complaint. Rules can differ significantly between state and federal courts and even between individual courts within these systems. These rules include the way to request a jury trial.

11. *Make sure you file in the correct court.* This means that the court in which you file the complaint must have personal jurisdiction over

the defendant, and subject matter jurisdiction over the dispute, and must be a proper venue.

▼ **Personal jurisdiction:** A court must have authority to assert its power over a defendant if it is to make a ruling impacting that defendant's rights. The ability of a court to assert personal jurisdiction over a particular defendant is defined by statutes and case law applicable in that jurisdiction. Traditionally, personal jurisdiction analysis requires that the defendant have some relationship with the state in which the court sits. Note, however, that a few federal statutes permit jurisdiction over defendants in cases brought under the statute in any federal district court in the United States. When deciding where to file suit, you should research personal jurisdiction to ensure that the court has jurisdiction over the defendant. It is a wise practice to plead facts in the complaint that establish personal jurisdiction over the defendant.

▼ **Subject matter jurisdiction:** Federal and state statutes govern the types of cases particular courts may hear. For example, the state court system in a particular state may have specific courts to hear family law matters (such as divorces, divorce settlement, and child custody and support issues) and other general jurisdiction courts. In such states, only the family law courts have jurisdiction to hear family law matters; the other courts of general jurisdiction do not. Similarly, federal district courts have subject matter jurisdiction over federal questions (issues governed by federal law) and disputes between citizens of different states if the amount in controversy exceeds a statutorily defined threshold. You should review the subject matter jurisdiction statutes applicable to the court system in which you plan to file a complaint to ensure that the complaint is filed in the proper court. Moreover, when drafting the complaint, you should plead adequate facts to establish that the court in which the complaint will be filed has subject matter jurisdiction over the dispute.

▼ **Venue:** In some ways, venue is related to subject matter jurisdiction, but it is a distinct concept and its requirements must be met. Venue requirements also are governed by statute and relate to the place the suit may be brought. The intent of venue statutes is to ensure that the suit is brought in a convenient forum. A complaint should include allegations establishing that the suit is brought in a proper venue.

12. *Make sure you name all proper defendants.* Sometimes this is easier said than done. For example, corporate or business relationships can make determining the proper party to sue difficult. Say you are filing a suit

based on a product your client purchased that does not work. Do you sue the seller, the manufacturer, the distributor, or some combination of the above? The best course of action is to review all documents associated with the transaction to determine which entities have played a role in the facts that form the basis of the suit and to name all defendants for which there is a good faith basis for doing so. But also consider who is within the jurisdiction of the court you prefer, who has the ability to pay if you prevail, and whether your client would prefer not to sue a particular party in order to preserve a relationship.

13.   *Reread and edit.* Set the complaint aside for a day and then reread it. Most likely you will find that some areas are not as clear as they could be. Another way to test the effectiveness of the complaint is to ask a colleague with no knowledge of the case to read the complaint and give her reaction.

14.   *Take all required actions with filing.* A court may reject your complaint because you failed to include a civil cover sheet required by the local rules, a filing fee, or an "interested parties" disclosure form, for example. This is embarrassing and potentially serious if the statute of limitations expires before you can re-file. Make sure to check local rules and the court's web site for filing guidelines.

15.   *Serve the complaint properly.* Upon filing a complaint, the clerk of the court will issue a summons that must be served on the defendant along with the complaint. Unless the defendant agrees to waive formal service in writing, the complaint and summons must be served on the defendant (not his lawyer) through a procedure called "service of process." Service of process is the means by which a court obtains personal jurisdiction over a defendant, so the court must have statutory authorization to assert that jurisdiction over the defendant through its process. Service of process is discussed more fully in Chapter 9.[1]

   ▼   Note that the time to answer a complaint generally does not begin to run until process has been served on the defendant. Under the rules of many courts, the amount of time a defendant has to answer depends on the means of service of process. For example, under the Federal Rules, a defendant may receive additional time to respond to the complaint if it waived formal service of process.

---

[1] Note that "service of process" is different from serving documents in ongoing litigation. In general, documents in litigation may be served on other parties by providing a copy to the parties' counsel and attaching a "Certificate of Service" indicating how the document was sent (via mail, for example) and the date it was sent. This is often referred to as "service" and is distinct from "service of process."

Accordingly, you must know the means by which process was served and the date of that service in order to determine when an answer (or Motion to Dismiss) is due.

A sample "barebones" complaint is attached as Exhibit A, and a sample detailed complaint is attached as Exhibit B. ➤

CHAPTER 4

Drafting Answers

Answers respond to complaints by replying to each factual allegation asserted in the complaint. The answer also must set forth any affirmative defenses, counterclaims, and cross-claims.

The content of the answer is driven by the allegations of the complaint. Because the answer simply responds to the allegations of the complaint by admitting or denying them, strategic issues play less of a role in drafting the answer. Whether to answer, as opposed to filing a Motion to Dismiss, however, is an important consideration.

TIPS AND SUGGESTIONS

1. *Notify the client of its obligation to preserve all evidence, regardless of its standard policies.* As soon as a party knows that litigation is likely, it should begin preserving all relevant evidence. This is the same notice process as is conducted prior to filing a complaint. If the client has a policy of regularly destroying documents or deleting electronic files, these practices should be suspended. Jurisdictions and local rules vary regarding the consequences of destroying documents after litigation is likely or has commenced, so check applicable law. In any case, ask your assigning attorney if the following steps are appropriate:

   ▼ Notify the client contact (usually a high-level employee such as the general counsel) of the obligation to preserve evidence.

   ▼ Send a memo to all company employees and others who may have relevant evidence (such as documents and e-mails) asking to preserve it.

   ▼ Ask the company's information technology department to preserve any back-up tapes or the like.

2. *Confirm the facts.* Before drafting an answer, confirm that the responses to be provided in the answer are accurate.

Take the following steps prior to filing the answer:

▼ Gather and review all relevant documents.

▼ Interview your client and potential witnesses. Interviews tell you what people know and who else you should interview.

▼ Are there any arbitration clauses implicated by the claim(s)? Can your client demand that the case be heard in an arbitration, as opposed to a court? Should your client do so?

▼ Consider whether the asserted claims trigger insurance coverage for your client.

3. *Determine if the defendant should "answer" or file a motion.* Certain legal defenses may be waived if the defendant responds to the complaint by filing an answer, rather than a Motion to Dismiss. Defenses that may be waived include lack of personal jurisdiction or improper venue. Motions to Dismiss are discussed in more detail in Chapter 7.

Immediately upon receiving the assignment to draft the answer, ask the assigning attorney if you should research the following questions in order to determine if you should file an answer (as opposed to a Motion to Dismiss):

▼ Does the court have jurisdiction over your client?

▼ Did the plaintiff file the case in the proper court? In other words, does the court have subject matter jurisdiction over the case, and is venue proper?

▼ If the case is filed in state court, is there a basis for federal jurisdiction? If so, should you remove the case from state court to federal court? Should you answer the claim first? Can you preserve certain aspects of state substantive law if you do so? Because removal is not a right that defendants lose if they fail to invoke it before answering, you may choose to wait before removing. In any event, discuss these issues with a senior attorney. Issues to discuss include whether there is any advantage to being in federal court as opposed to state court.

▼ Which legal defenses does the defendant have to the complaint? Must any of those defenses be asserted prior to filing an answer?

▼ Has the plaintiff adequately pled the factual elements of each of its causes of action?

Your answers to these questions will determine whether you should recommend that your client file a motion as opposed to an answer.

4. *If you decide to file an answer, there generally are four possible responses to each paragraph in the complaint:* (i) admit, (ii) deny, (iii) assert a lack of

information (which is treated as a denial), or (iv) note that the paragraph contains a legal conclusion to which no response is required.

DENIALS There are three types of denials: general denials, specific denials, and qualified specific denials.

General denials. General denials deny each and every allegation in the complaint, including those of jurisdiction. The Federal Rules and the rules of some state courts permit them. A general denial consists of a short statement that "the defendant denies all allegations of the complaint." A general denial gives the defendant flexibility in asserting arguments later but provides no opportunity to immediately counter the plaintiff's allegations. General denials may be asserted only if the defendant has a good faith basis for denying each and every allegation in the complaint.

Specific denials. A specific denial specifically denies a particular paragraph of the complaint. For example, a specific denial would state that "defendant denies the allegations of paragraph 4 of the complaint."

Qualified specific denials. A qualified specific denial permits the defendant to except certain portions of a paragraph from a specific denial of that paragraph. For example, if paragraph 3 of a complaint alleged that "Walker Johnson, Inc. is a Virginia corporation with its principal place of business in Sterling, Virginia," the defendant could respond that "the defendant admits that Walker Johnson, Inc. is a Virginia corporation but denies the remaining allegations of paragraph 3 of the complaint."

LACK OF KNOWLEDGE "Lack of Knowledge" has the effect of a denial. If, for example, the defendant in good faith lacks sufficient information to form a belief as to the accuracy of the allegations in a paragraph, the defendant can allege that it "is without sufficient information or knowledge to admit or deny the allegations in paragraph 2 and therefore denies the allegations and demands strict proof thereof."

ADMISSIONS If any facts pled in the complaint are true, the defendant must admit them. Admissions should be clear as to what the defendant admits. Thus, rather than simply responding "admit," the defendant should state that it "admits the allegations in paragraph 3 of the complaint," or that it "admits that Walker Johnson, Inc. is a Virginia corporation with its principal place of business in Ashburn, Virginia."

5. *Do not miss the deadline.* In general, the Federal Rules give defendants 20 days from the date of service of the complaint and summons to file a response to the complaint. However, you must consult the local rules to confirm the deadline because those rules and the method of service may

alter it. If the defendant fails to file an answer (or a Motion to Dismiss) within the time allowed, the plaintiff may move for default. Under the local rules of many courts, the deadline date is the date the document must be received by the clerk's office, not the date by which it must be mailed. Also, note that although opposing counsel may agree to provide an extension of time, that extension may not be effective unless it is formally approved by court order. In other courts, the parties may only have to provide the court with a joint stipulation or letter for the extension to be effective.

6. *Note that a verified complaint may require a verified answer.* As with a verified complaint, a verified answer includes an oath that the responses therein are true and accurate to the best of the knowledge and belief of the person taking the oath. Allow more time to prepare a verified answer, since your client will need to review it carefully.

7. *Do not respond to only part of the complaint.* Any allegations the responding party does not answer may be deemed to have been admitted.

8. *Plead all applicable affirmative defenses.* Failure to raise an affirmative defense in the answer may result in waiver of that defense. Affirmative defenses are identified in separate paragraphs in the answer that should be labeled "Affirmative Defenses" after the responses to the allegations in the plaintiff's complaint. Ask the assigning attorney which affirmative defenses to assert, and research the plaintiff's causes of action to determine which defenses are commonly asserted against them. Common affirmative defenses that must be pled in the answer include:

   ▼ accord and satisfaction;
   ▼ arbitration and award;
   ▼ assumption of risk;
   ▼ contributory negligence;
   ▼ discharge in bankruptcy;
   ▼ duress;
   ▼ estoppel;
   ▼ failure of consideration;
   ▼ fraud;
   ▼ illegality;
   ▼ injury by fellow servant;
   ▼ laches;
   ▼ license;
   ▼ payment;

▼ release;

▼ res judicata;

▼ statute of frauds;

▼ statute of limitations; and

▼ waiver.

There are many more affirmative defenses potentially available under state law. Remember that there must be a good faith basis for asserting each affirmative defense.

9. *Learn the judge's background.* Find a biography and copies of published opinions (or ask your firm librarian to do so). Give copies to your assigning attorney.

10. *Consider a jury demand.* Research whether the claims the plaintiff alleged permit a jury trial, and, in consultation with a more experienced attorney, consider whether a jury trial would be advantageous to your client.

11. *Consider counterclaims, cross-claims, and third-party claims.* A *counterclaim* is a claim by the defendant against the plaintiff and may be useful because it may place the plaintiff on the defensive and provide the defendant with a bargaining chip in settlement negotiations. Some counterclaims will be waived if not raised immediately. These are "compulsory" counterclaims.

A compulsory counterclaim:

▼ Exists at the time the answer is filed and is not asserted in other litigation;

▼ Arises from the same "transaction or occurrence" as the complaint; and

▼ Does not require that third parties be brought into the lawsuit.

Research the law in the jurisdiction and the court where the complaint is filed to determine if there are any compulsory counterclaims. Non-compulsory counterclaims are called "permissive counterclaims." Permissive counterclaims are not waived if they are not asserted in the answer.

Cross-claims and *third-party claims* are claims against fellow defendants. Cross-claims are brought against existing defendants in the same case; third-party claims are brought against new defendants that the defendant, acting as a third-party plaintiff, brings into the suit.

12. *Include a request for relief and demand for judgment* on the affirmative defenses asserted and any counterclaims, cross-claims, or third-party claims.

13. *Consult the local rules.* Before filing your answer, review all applicable rules to ensure that the answer fully complies with them. Also, if you are filing the answer by some method other than hand delivery to the court, allow time for mailing so that the answer is filed on time.

A sample answer is attached as Exhibit C. ❖

CHAPTER 5

Conducting and Making Discovery

GENERAL

Discovery is the process of collecting and producing the information and documents relevant to a case. The facts necessary to support the legal theories, claims, and defenses are found (or not found) in discovery.

Because discovery brings junior associates closest to the facts, it is an opportunity for junior associates to make themselves indispensable to more senior attorneys. New attorneys conducting discovery are asked to process and know a huge volume of information. The vastness and tedium of some discovery assignments makes mistakes easy. It is in discovery that a junior associate can make a notorious litigation mistake: accidentally sending a privileged document to the opposing party.

In discovery, junior associates are often assigned to:

► Draft discovery requests.

► Respond to discovery requests.

► Review, analyze, and produce documents to the adverse party.

► Review and analyze the documents produced by the adverse party.

As a junior associate, you must master the information obtained in discovery. Senior attorneys on the case will rely on you as an expert on the facts of the case and the progress of discovery itself.

Summary of the Discovery Process

In many cases, including those governed by the Federal Rules, discovery proceeds as follows:

1. The court sets a scheduling conference.
2. The parties meet and confer regarding the discovery process in the case at least twenty-one days before the scheduling conference is to occur.

The goal of that "meet and confer" session is for the parties to agree on a schedule to present to the judge at the scheduling conference. Because the plaintiff usually wants a long discovery period and the defendant a short one, judges often must resolve scheduling disputes at the conference.

3. The parties make their Initial Disclosures. See the description of these under item 5 of "Tips and Suggestions."

4. The parties attend the scheduling conference and the judge establishes the schedule for discovery.

5. Discovery commences. Once discovery begins, you may serve written discovery requests on counsel for the other parties. These might include interrogatories and requests for production of documents, for example. You also may receive written discovery from the other parties.

TIPS AND SUGGESTIONS

1. *Develop a proof plan.* A proof plan identifies the facts and information that your client needs to make its case against the other party (or to defend against the other party's claims). If you represent the plaintiff, you should develop a proof plan before the complaint is filed. Defendants' lawyers should develop a proof plan as soon as they receive the complaint. A proof plan should list the causes of action in the complaint, the element of each cause of action, and the elements of each defense (drawn from the relevant statutes, cases, and/or model jury instructions). For each element of each cause of action and defense, the proof plan should list the following:

    ▼ The evidence you have or expect to obtain to (dis)prove it.

    ▼ The method(s) of discovery by which you will obtain each such piece of evidence (e.g., deposition, interrogatory, request for production).

    ▼ The method by which you will establish the admissibility of each such piece of the evidence at trial.

    ▼ The witnesses you intend to depose and the information you need from each witness.

    Review, supplement, and update the proof plan on a regular basis. A sample proof plan is attached as Exhibit D. ➝

2. *Develop a discovery plan.* If your client is a company or other entity, an employee will be responsible for discovery information. Often this person would rather do his own work than handle your requests for more information and more documents, so you should assure him that you will respect his time. It helps if you agree with your client on a plan in

advance. This may increase the client's cooperation and will help control how many requests you must make of him. A sample discovery plan is attached as Exhibit E. ➥

3. *Critically analyze the documents and information provided by your client.* In litigation, your client likely will be required to deliver all relevant files to the opposing party. Collect and analyze all documents (and interview all witnesses) as early as possible so that you know all information that will go to the other side. Senior attorneys cannot competently advise a client on the litigation risks and potential and likely outcome of the litigation if they do not know what information lies in the client's files. Also, you should know if there are documents in the client's files that will hurt its public image and, thus, its business. Is there a document the disclosure of which would embarrass your client and bring an avalanche of "copy cat" suits? If so, advise your supervising attorney immediately so that she can evaluate whether a quick settlement is warranted.

4. *"Bates" number documents to be produced.* "Bates" numbering involves stamping an identifying prefix and numbers on documents prior to producing them. For example, the first document produced by ABC Corporation might be labeled with "ABC00001," with each consecutive page identified with the next number in the series (ABC00002, ABC00003, etc.). Before affixing "Bates" numbers to the documents, remove documents that are privileged or otherwise exempt from production. This avoids awkward gaps in the "Bates" numbers. Create a separate series of "Bates" numbers for privileged documents and begin each of those with "PRIV" before the number. When producing documents to another party, note the range of documents by their "Bates" number in a cover letter so that you have a record of the documents that have been produced and the date(s) on which they were produced.

5. *Obtain all relevant discovery from the other side as soon as possible.* No one knows the merits of a case until she has reviewed all of the evidence. Even inadmissible evidence can be obtained in discovery if it is relevant and "reasonably calculated" to lead to the discovery of admissible evidence. The first materials you should receive from the opposing part are its Initial Disclosures.

INITIAL DISCLOSURES Initial Disclosures are now mandated by the Federal Rules and require that each party disclose the following, early in the litigation, without waiting for a discovery request from an adverse party:

▶   **Witnesses:** the name, address, and telephone number of each individual likely to have discoverable information, and identification of the subjects of information possessed by each such person.

▶ **Documents:** a description, or copy, of all documents in the possession, custody, or control of the party that may be used to support its claims or defenses.

▶ **Damages:** a computation of damages and the documents or other materials on which that computation is made (unless privileged) and documents relevant to the nature and extent of the injuries suffered.

▶ **Insurance:** any insurance agreement, the proceeds of which may be used to satisfy all or a part of any judgment entered in the action.

The Initial Disclosures should be made in writing, signed by counsel of record, served on all parties, and filed with the court unless the local rules provide otherwise. If a party fails to disclose certain supporting information and/or documents in the Initial Disclosures (or a subsequent supplement thereto), that party may be precluded from relying on them in the case.

6. *Do not waive privileges.* Evidentiary privileges provide one party with the right not to disclose certain information to the other party. As a junior associate, you are entrusted with privileged documents. If you accidentally send privileged documents or information to opposing parties, your client may lose the privilege and you may be responsible for that loss. In many jurisdictions, inadvertent production of a privileged document results in waiver of the privilege with respect to that particular document and any other privileged documents covering the same subject matter.

BACKGROUND ON PRIVILEGES Generally, matters protected by a privilege are not subject to disclosure in discovery. However, courts construe privileges narrowly.

If a party relies on a privilege as a basis for non-disclosure in discovery, that party must provide sufficient information about the information that is withheld to permit the party requesting the discovery to evaluate the assertion of privilege. For documents, this is usually done in a "privilege log" identifying each document withheld on the basis of privilege and providing enough information about the document to demonstrate that it is privileged (such as author, recipient, and general subject matter). Privileges must be asserted on a question-by-question or a document-by-document basis. If only a portion of a document is protected from disclosure by a privilege, that portion should be redacted (blacked-out), but the rest of the document must be disclosed.

Most privileges are defined by state, as opposed to federal, law. Common privileges include the attorney-client privilege and the work product doctrine, the doctor-patient privilege, the accountant privilege (in some, but not all, jurisdictions), and marital privilege. The privilege against self-incrimination and governmental privileges (such as executive privilege) are two federal privileges.

All of these privileges are subject to waiver and exceptions, which also are defined by law. For example, an assertion of most privileges may be overcome by demonstrating that the allegedly privileged information was disclosed to persons not subject to the privilege. An assertion of work product may be overcome by demonstrating a substantial need for the information and the inability to get it from another source.

TIPS FOR AVOIDING ACCIDENTAL DISCLOSURE OF PRIVILEGED MATERIAL

Take great care in protecting and maintaining privileges. Consider the following precautions:

► Obtain a list from the client of the names of all their attorneys and other legal staff (such as paralegals). When reviewing documents for privilege, always check the names appearing in the documents against this list. Also, if you are unsure of whether someone referenced in the document is an attorney, check with the client.

► If you are not sure if a document is privileged, consult the author and/or recipient before you produce it.

► Whenever you receive any client documents, immediately separate all that are privileged.

► Store privileged documents in a separate file.

► "Bates" number (see item 4 of "Tips and Suggestions" under "Conducting and Making Discovery") privileged documents with the "PRIV" prefix and a number to keep track of them.

► Before producing a document, personally review the documents to be provided to ensure that no documents with a "PRIV" label are included. Then ask a paralegal or secretary to double-check your review.

If you inadvertently send privileged material to the other side:

▼ Tell the senior lawyers immediately.

▼ Request that the other side return it and any copies that were made.

▼ Research how the court in which the litigation is pending treats inadvertent disclosure and take any steps suggested by the research to mitigate the inadvertent disclosure.

7. *Make sure to include a Certificate of Service on all documents that you serve on the opposing party.* A Certificate of Service is a document attached to any documents you serve on the opposing party that identifies the person on whom the document was served, the date of service, and the method of service. The date on your Certificate of Service will determine when response time for the party receiving the document begins to run. A Certificate of Service also may serve as presumptive evidence that the persons identified received the document.

Respond to a failure to provide discovery and inform senior attorneys of this failure immediately. Consider that you may be able to resolve a discovery failure and protect your client as follows:

► As soon as an opposing party has failed to provide discovery or has provided responses you believe to be inadequate, arrange a telephone conference to discuss your concerns.

► If the opposing party agrees to provide the requested discovery, be sure to set a deadline.

► Follow this conversation with a letter documenting your concerns and the response of the opposing party.

► If the opposing party still does not cure the deficiencies of its discovery responses, arrange another meeting and advise counsel that you intend to file a Motion to Compel Discovery if the deficiencies are not corrected.

► Again, this meeting should be followed by a letter documenting what occurred.

► Establish your good faith efforts to resolve the dispute. This will be important to winning your motion to compel discovery. See Chapter 7 for a discussion of Motions to Compel Discovery.

The primary methods of discovery—interrogatories, requests for production of documents, requests for admissions, and depositions—are discussed below.

INTERROGATORIES

Interrogatories allow one party to pose written questions to another party. The responding party must answer the interrogatories in writing under oath and/or object to them. Because interrogatories are generally answered by lawyers (rather than parties themselves), some lawyers do not consider interrogatories to be especially revealing. But others say that they can be used to expand the information provided in the Initial Disclosures, to learn more about the claims and defenses asserted, and to require the adverse party to take a position, thereby boxing that party into the position.

TIPS AND SUGGESTIONS

1. *Use interrogatories wisely.* There is a limit of twenty-five interrogatories per party under the Federal Rules (inclusive of "subparts," which is not defined). Do not use interrogatories to request information that can be obtained another way, such as by the Initial Disclosures or requests for production of documents (which generally are unlimited). If your client is served more than twenty-five interrogatories, consider answering the first twenty-five and objecting to the remainder (but first ensure that your jurisdiction allows this without waiving the objection for excessive interrogatories).

2. *Use carefully considered instructions and definitions.* Interrogatories should contain a section with instructions and definitions that identify the relevant period of time for responsive information, define terms used in the interrogatories (such as "document") and provide instructions to the responding party if information is privileged or is not available. Some jurisdictions maintain mandatory model instructions and definitions in their local rules, others have permissible model instructions and definitions, while still others provide no model. In any case, do not hesitate to supplement model instructions and definitions if necessary and appropriate.

3. *When responding to a set of interrogatories, ask yourself why your client is being asked each question.* This may provide insight into the adverse party's strategy. Discuss this with the assigning attorney. Note all applicable objections to each request. Also indicate if privileged information is withheld. Remember that responses to interrogatories (but not objections, if served separately) are signed under oath by the client, so take care with the responses.

4. *Consult your proof plan, complaint, and answer for facts and information you need to obtain by interrogatories.* Do not limit your interrogatories to information that supports only your client's claims or defenses—you want to know everything on which the other party may rely at trial.

5. *Do not reinvent the wheel.* Ask the assigning attorney whether she has a set of interrogatories (or models for responses) from a similar case to help you begin your drafting.

6. *Use information-seeking and contention interrogatories. Information-seeking interrogatories* should be used to get facts (who, what, when, where, and how) and identifications (documents, witnesses, experts, etc.). *Contention interrogatories* should be used to require the adverse party to state its position on an issue or to explain the basis for a contention, but they cannot require the adverse party to provide a statement of pure law.

7. *Require the plaintiff to show damages.* If the plaintiff failed to articulate its damages in the complaint, consider asking it to do so through an interrogatory. Surprisingly often, plaintiffs fail to provide a meaningful response. This can be used to the defendant's advantage at summary judgment or at trial.

8. *Consult the local rules.* Before serving your interrogatories, review all applicable rules. Also, do not forget to file in court a notice that discovery has been served if required by the local rules and to include a Certificate of Service on the discovery.[1]

A sample set of interrogatories is attached as Exhibit G. ➤

REQUESTS FOR PRODUCTION AND INSPECTION

Requests for Production can seek inspection of documents, land, or things such as automobiles (in a breach of warranty case against an automobile manufacturer, for example). Local rules often contain rules and limitations on the use of requests for production and inspection. Requests for production must be directed toward parties to the litigation. However, discovery of documents from nonparties is available by subpoena.

TIPS AND SUGGESTIONS

1. *Use a request for production instead of an interrogatory, if possible.* Unlike interrogatories, the Federal Rules do not set a firm limit on the number of requests for production a party can pose under the Federal Rules.

2. *Include carefully considered instructions and definitions.* Requests for production or inspection should contain a section with instructions and definitions that set the timeframe for responsive information, define terms used in the requests (such as "document" or "property"), and

---

[1] A Certificate of Service is a document attached to any documents you serve on the opposing party that identifies the person on whom the document was served, the date of service, and the method of service. A sample Certificate of Service is attached as Exhibit F.

provide instructions to the responding party if material is privileged or not available. Some jurisdictions maintain mandatory model instructions and definitions in their local rules, others have permissible model instructions and definitions, while still others provide no model. In any case, do not hesitate to supplement model instructions and definitions if necessary and appropriate.

3. *When responding to requests for production and inspection, consider why you are being asked for documents or inspection.* This may provide insight into the adverse party's strategy. Discuss this with the assigning attorney. Note all applicable objections to each request. Also, indicate that privileged documents are withheld.

4. *Consult your proof plan, complaint, and answer for documents you need to obtain by a Request for Production.* Do not limit your Requests for Production or inspections to materials that support only your client's claims or defenses—you want to know everything on which the other party may rely at trial.

5. *Do not reinvent the wheel.* Document requests from past cases also may provide ideas about the types of documents to request. Document requests prepared by the senior attorney on the case (or associates who work for him/her) also may provide ideas.

6. *Consult the local rules.* Before serving your Requests for Production, review all applicable rules to ensure that the requests fully comply with them. In addition, do not forget to file in court a notice that discovery has been served, if required by the local rules, and to include a Certificate of Service when you serve the requests.

A sample Request for Production and Inspection is attached as Exhibit H.[2] ⟶

REQUESTS FOR ADMISSION

Requests for Admission should be used to establish that certain facts are not disputed and thereby narrowing the issues to be litigated. Once a fact is admitted, a court may permit a party to withdraw or amend its admission.

The Federal Rules do not limit the number of Requests for Admission, but the local rules of some courts do.

---

[2] A Certificate of Service is a document attached to any documents you serve on the opposing party that identifies the person on whom the document was served, the date of service, and the method of service. A sample Certificate of Service is attached as Exhibit F.

TIPS AND SUGGESTIONS

1. *Do not request that another party admit disputed issues.* Requests for Admission on disputed issues serve no purpose because the responding party may either deny the request or state that the issue is in dispute.

2. *Be clear and direct.* Each request should contain only one fact or issue to be admitted and should not contain argument. Explanation, multiple facts, and argument increase the chance that the receiving party will have a basis to deny the request.

3. *Phrase the request carefully.* If the Request for Admission is relevant to an element of claim or defense in the case (and in the proof plan), make sure the language of the request mirrors the language of that element. If you do not, you may not be able to use the admission at trial to establish an element of your proof.

4. *Confirm receipt of the requests.* If a party does not respond to a Request for Admission within the allowed time, that request may be deemed admitted. However, you should establish that the opposing party's counsel received the request. Send the requests by a method of delivery through which you can confirm receipt, and/or to follow service with a faxed letter to opposing counsel. This may prevent opposing counsel from subsequently denying receipt of the requests.

5. *When providing an admission, ask yourself why the other side would want your client to make the requested admission.* This may provide insight into that party's strategy. Discuss your conclusions with the assigning attorney. Remember that admissions may be binding, so be certain about the admissions you make.

6. *Consult the local rules.* Before serving your requests for production, review all applicable rules. Also, do not forget to file in court a notice that discovery has been served, if required by the local rules, and to include a Certificate of Service.[3]

    A sample Request for Admission is attached as Exhibit I.

---

[3] A Certificate of Service is a document attached to any documents you serve on the opposing party that identifies the person on whom the document was served, the date of service, and the method of service. A sample Certificate of Service is attached as Exhibit F.

ORAL DEPOSITIONS

A deposition is testimony of a party or a nonparty that is taken under oath outside a courtroom. During a trial, a witness' deposition transcript is useful in cross-examining that witness and, if possible, in impeaching him.

Assume that you will be asked to take or defend a deposition early in your career so that you are ready when the opportunity arises.

Purposes of Deposition

Depositions can have various purposes. Among those purposes are:

1. Fact investigation and fact gathering.
2. Protecting the record before the witnesses can coordinate their stories.
3. Demonstrating that the witness is not knowledgeable about the facts, is unreliable, or is not credible.
4. Pitting parties against one another (if it is helpful to do so in a multiparty case). For example, the deposition of one defendant in a car accident gives that defendant an opportunity to circulate information about what other defendants did wrong. This may cause the co-defendants to point their fingers at each other (and assert cross-claims). If the defendants attack one another and point out what other defendants did wrong, the plaintiff benefits.
5. Assessing what impact the witness would have at trial.
6. Sending a message to the opposing party regarding settlement.

Prior to the deposition, you and the assigning attorney must decide which of these purposes you seek to accomplish. But be prepared to change course and accomplish other goals during the deposition if the witness has other valuable informtion.

Who May Be Deposed? How Does the Process Work?

► Although only parties with an interest in the litigation may take a deposition in a case, both parties and non-parties may be deposed.

► Deposing a party in a case only requires serving a "Notice of Deposition."[4] However, deposing a non-party requires serving that person with a subpoena (or getting that person to agree to appear voluntarily for deposition without a subpoena, as discussed below).

---

[4] A sample Notice of Deposition is attached as Exhibit J.

▶ Nonparty deponents may agree to appear for a deposition voluntarily or voluntarily accept informal service of a subpoena (no one likes having a process server show up at their job), so consider contacting a nonparty deponent (or her counsel) prior to serving subpoena by a process server to see if the deponent (or her attorney) will accept service of the subpoena.

▶ You also may require a nonparty to produce documents pursuant to a subpoena duces tecum.

▶ Entities can be deposed as well as people. Under the Federal Rules, Rule 30(b)(6) permits the deposition of a corporation, partnership, association, or governmental agency. In a 30(b)(6) deposition, a representative of the entity is appointed to answer questions on its behalf concerning issues specified in the notice and must be educated about the entity's knowledge of those issues.

Preparing a Witness for Deposition

▶ Meet with your client close to the deposition date, but allow a window of time between the meeting and the deposition in case you need more time to address any issues that arise during the meeting.

▶ Do not prepare a witness in a room with other witnesses or non-attorneys; doing so may waive the attorney-client privilege.

▶ Do not advertise to the witness that this is your first deposition, but do not deny it either. You might ask senior lawyers how to handle this question if asked by your client. If pressed, you could say that you "have been training to take depositions for several years" (which, with law school, is the truth).

▶ Begin the preparation session by giving an overview of the deposition process.

▶ Advise the deponent of the following ground rules for depositions:

1. Always tell the truth.

2. Listen carefully to each question. Feel free to ask the questioning attorney to repeat it.

3. After each question is asked, briefly pause so that your lawyer has time to object.

4. Only answer the question asked. Do not volunteer information or explain or expand on your answer unless asked to do so. Do not guess or speculate as to what other people know. If you do not know or cannot recall the answer, do not speculate or guess; just say "I do not know" or "I do not recall" (but remind the client of the difference between these).

5. Speak for yourself.

  ▼ If asked a series of questions and then asked for a conclusion, try to summarize the answers to the prior questions when providing the conclusion.

  For example, if, after a series of questions about what the defendant was doing immediately prior to a car accident, the deposing attorney says "So if I understand your testimony, you were running late and in a hurry because you got in a big argument with your husband before you left for work that day, is that correct," rather than simply responding "Yes," the defendant-deponent should say "It is true that we got in a fight that delayed me, but I was driving carefully and was not speeding."

  ▼ Do not let the questioning attorney put words in your mouth.

  ▼ Do not let the questioning attorney interrupt or cut off your answers. If he attempts to do so, ask to finish your answer.

  ▼ Finally, if the questioning attorney attempts to limit you by stating "Have you told me everything you know about x, y, and z," be sure to respond that you have "stated everything I remember right now."

6. Do not exaggerate or speak in absolutes unless warranted. Ask for clarification of any words or questions you do not understand.

▶ Assess the witness' knowledge. Go over everything the witness knows that is relevant to the case. This provides a forecast of their testimony and jogs their memory. Ask open-ended questions and follow up with specific questions until you have covered everything. Remember that the substance of your preparation session is discoverable if it serves to refresh the deponent's recollection as to any facts or issues, so take care that you do not disclose litigation strategy to the deponent.

▶ Finally, review with the witness any documents about which you expect him to be asked.

TIPS AND SUGGESTIONS

1. *Use depositions wisely; interview.* The Federal Rules contain a presumptive limit of ten depositions of seven hours each per side. If there are multiple parties on the same side of the dispute (e.g., three co-defendants), those parties must divide the depositions. Taking more depositions requires a party to obtain leave (permission) of court or reach agreement with the other party. Party witnesses ordinarily may not speak to opposing counsel

voluntarily without a deposition, so you must use depositions to determine what they know. However, before you use depositions on non-party witnesses who may be willing to speak with you, consider interviewing them to see if they are worth deposing. Then you can determine what they know, whether they will testify at trial, and whether you need a deposition to preserve their testimony under oath.

2. *Prepare.*

    ▼   Understand the case and how your deponent fits into it.

    ▼   Meet with senior attorneys to get their thoughts and advice about the deposition.

    ▼   Review notes from any witness interviews.

    ▼   Review very thoroughly the allegations and causes of action alleged in the complaint, as well as any affirmative defenses and counterclaims.

    ▼   Bring copies of relevant pleadings, such as the complaint, answer, and discovery responses, to the deposition.

    ▼   Analyze interrogatory responses and documents for ways in which they support or refute the claims. Always go into a deposition knowing everything about the facts and documents that can be known at that stage.

3. *Decide on your objectives for the deposition.* Do you want to know what poster was on the CEO's wall? Do you want to know the day on which a conversation took place? Decide your goals in advance. If you are hoping to gain testimony to use in a summary judgment motion, picture the deponent's responses as a quotation in the motion. If the answer is not phased in a useful manner, ask the question again in a different way. This is why questions are often repeated in depositions: to get the answer that the questioner seeks in the most useful form.

4. *Plan your inquiry.*

    ▼   Use your proof plan to prepare an outline of the substantive issues and areas you need to cover with each witness to be deposed. Your outline can be organized by the legal issues, claims, or chronologically.

    ▼   Note the documents that need to be authenticated with each witness. Authentication provides the evidentiary basis for the admissibility of a document. If you plan to offer a document produced by the other side in support of a motion for summary judgment, for example, you may need deposition testimony establishing the authenticity and bases for admissibility of the document. (Note that it may be possible to use requests of admission to establish the authenticity and admissibility of a document.)

▼ Keep the documents you will use in the deposition arranged in the order you plan to use them and place a reference to these documents in your outline so that you do not forget about them.

▼ Write out your questions (at least the key questions) and show these to the senior lawyers in advance. The phrasing of these questions is important to getting the answer you need. But do not blindly adhere to your written list. Keep alert for additional questions and/or new areas of inquiry.

5. *Notice the deposition of party witnesses.* The deposition of a party may require serving that party's counsel with a Notice of Deposition.[5] Check the local rules and any orders by the judge assigned to the case. Generally, a deposition notice must provide:

▼ **Reasonable notice.** The deposition notice must provide each party with reasonable notice of the deposition. "Reasonable notice" will be determined based on the facts and circumstances of the case, but, as a general rule, it is advisable to provide notice of the deposition a week or two in advance, unless you previously discussed the date of the deposition with counsel for the other parties.

▼ **When.** The deposition must provide the date and hour of the deposition. It is best to coordinate with the deponent's counsel to find a convenient time.

▼ **Where.** The notice must state where the deposition will be taken. It is best to confer with the deponent's counsel to find a mutually agreeable place for the deposition. However, you should also be aware of applicable court rules governing where depositions must occur in absence of consent from the deponent and counsel for all parties.

▼ **Who.** The notice must provide the name and address of the person to be examined.

▼ **How.** The notice must provide the method by which the testimony will be recorded (e.g., stenographically, by video, etc).

For a 30(b)(6) deposition, the notice also must provide the areas of inquiry and state that the entity to be deposed has a duty to designate a qualified person to testify as to those areas.

Do not forget to file in court a notice that discovery has been served if required by the local rules, and to include a Certificate of Service (a sample of which is attached as Exhibit F).

6. *If you have not discussed the deposition with counsel for the deponent prior to serving the notice, you should call that attorney or expect a call from him*

---

[5] A sample Notice of Deposition is attached as Exhibit J.

after serving the notice. Topics likely to be discussed during this call include scheduling (e.g., the deponent will be out of the country on the date you noticed) or setting some limitations on the deposition (e.g., the deponent must pick up his child from day care prior to 5 p.m., so he must leave by 4:15 p.m.). Discuss any issues raised in this call with your assigning attorney prior to making any commitments.

7. *Confirm logistics.* Make certain that you have confirmed the basic necessities:

   ▼ Arrange for a court reporter if you are taking the deposition (if you are defending the deposition, the party taking it should arrange for the court reporter).[6] Your supervisor probably has a favorite court reporter;

   ▼ Reserve a room for the deposition; and

   ▼ Ensure that non-party witnesses who were subpoenaed received the "witness fee" required by the subpoena and the applicable rules (the subpoena may be rendered invalid if it is not accompanied by the witness fee).

8. *Review and understand the rules.*

   ▼ Understand the evidentiary rules that apply in a deposition, which are different from the rules that apply in court For example, "calls for hearsay" is not a proper objection in a deposition. The evidentiary rules are discussed below.

   ▼ In some jurisdictions, a deponent may not confer with his attorney about the deposition—except to determine whether to assert a privilege—once he starts testifying. However, some lawyers do not insist on compliance with this rule, even where it does apply, figuring that they will want to confer with their own clients during deposition.

   ▼ Never go into a deposition without a copy of all applicable rules and/or cases that govern deposition procedure. The applicable rules may be those of the jurisdiction in which the deposition is taken, not the one where the case is pending.

9. *Be careful about stipulations.* After a witness is sworn, someone will generally ask if the parties agree to the "usual stipulations." Get a statement of all stipulations on the record. The following is a list of stipulations commonly requested:

   ▼ *Agreement to waive the witness' right to read and sign the deposition transcript.* You should not agree to this—stenographers often make mistakes.

---

[6] Get a reference for a good court reporter from one of the senior attorneys. If the court reporter misses important testimony or gets it wrong, the deposition may be rendered worthless and you may not get another chance with the witness.

▼ *Agreement to waive the requirement that the deponent sign the transcript in front of a notary.* This stipulation is helpful to the witness, and you generally should agree to it.

▼ *Agreement in a multiparty case that any counsel's objection inures to the benefit of all opposing counsel.* Unless it is clear that this will benefit your client, you should not agree to this.

▼ *Agreement that an instruction from counsel not to answer will be deemed the equivalent of the deponent's refusal to answer.* Without this stipulation, an attorney's instruction to a witness not to answer a question is not enough—you must ask questions to "certify" that the witness will, in fact, decline to answer the question (see below). If you fail to certify the question, it will be difficult to compel an answer from the witness later because you never established that the witness would not answer the question. A stipulation that the witness will take her attorney's advice on instructions not to answer avoids certification and saves time. However, if you think there is a chance that the witness may decline her attorney's advice and answer anyway, do not raise this issue and do not agree to the stipulation.

10. *Provide instructions to the witness on the record.* After the stenographer has sworn in the deponent, the person taking the deposition should provide the witness with general instructions about the deposition on the record, even if the witness was already so instructed by her counsel while preparing for the deposition. The following instructions are common:

▼ I am [name], counsel for [client] in a lawsuit between [plaintiff(s)] and [defendant(s)].

▼ You have been placed under oath, and, although you are not testifying in a courtroom in front of a judge today, the oath you have taken gives your testimony the same force and effect as if it was taken in a courtroom. Do you understand?

▼ This deposition is taken by [stipulation, notice, and/or subpoena] pursuant to the [applicable procedural rules]. It will be used for purposes of discovery, cross-examination at trial, and all other purposes permitted by law. Do you understand?

▼ There is a court reporter here recording my questions and your answers, which will be produced in writing. You will have an opportunity to read and sign the transcript and correct any errors where the transcript does not accurately reflect what you state today. Okay?

▼ If at any time you do not understand or hear my question, please let me know and I will rephrase or repeat it. Do you agree to do this?

▼ If you do not ask me to repeat or rephrase a question, and you answer it, I will assume that you heard and understood the question, and the transcript will reflect this. Do you agree?

▼ There is a court reporter here who will be taking down what you say. As a result, all of your answers must be verbal responses, not head nods or "uh-huhs." Do you agree to give verbal responses?

▼ Sometimes you may forget to give a verbal response, and that is okay. I will either point to the court reporter or ask you to state your answer. That will be your clue to give a verbal response. Okay?

▼ This is not a test, and I do not expect you to know the answer to every question I ask. I also don't want you to speculate; you should only tell me what you know. Accordingly, if you do not know the answer to a question, just tell me so and I will move on. Do you agree?

▼ You may want to anticipate my question and answer it before I finish asking the question. Because we need to have a record of questions and answers, you must wait until I finish my question. Do you agree?

▼ Similarly, I may think you are finished answering a question and ask my next question before you have completed your answer. If this happens, please let me know and I will allow you to complete your answer. If you do not stop me, I will assume, and the transcript will reflect, that the answer you provided was your full and complete answer. Do you understand?

▼ If at anytime you feel you need a comfort break, please let me know and I will be happy to break at the next appropriate opportunity. Okay?

▼ Do you understand each one of the rules and instructions I have just explained?

▼ Do you have any questions before we proceed?

11. *Phrase questions carefully.*

▼ When deposing a witness, remember that you are making a written record. Your questions should be clear and concise.

▼ Picture your question and the deponent's answer as written in the deposition transcript and quoted in your summary judgment motion—your question must be precise to get the exact answer you want.

▼ Use open-ended questions to elicit narrative responses. Then narrow questions to nail down the witness' testimony. All areas of inquiry should be followed up with a question that limits the deponent's ability to offer additional information at trial, such as "Do you remember anything else about that conversation that you have not already testified about?"

▼ Leading questions may only be asked if the witness is hostile or aligned with the opposing party.

12. *Dealing with instructions not to answer.* There are only three bases for an instruction not to answer a question in a deposition:

1) Preservation of a privilege;

2) Enforcement of a limitation set by the court; and

3) An appropriate suspension of a deposition.

Thus, instructions not to answer based on relevance, repetitious questions or an evidentiary basis (e.g., hearsay) are inappropriate.

In response to an instruction not to answer a question you should:

▼ Require opposing counsel to state the basis for the instruction on the record.

▼ Certify the question by establishing that the witness has the information necessary to answer the question and would have answered but for the lawyer's instruction.

▼ Inquire into the factual basis for the assertion of privilege. For example, if the deponent is instructed not to answer based on attorney-client privilege, ask questions designed to establish whether there was an attorney-client relationship and whether the witness seeking legal advice. Also, always ask whether anyone not covered by a privilege was present when the allegedly attorney-client privileged information was discussed.

▼ Determine whether the witness has taken any action that would result in waiver of the privilege (e.g., the deponent discussed the privileged information with her best friend).

13. *Dealing with objections.*

▼ All objections except those that can be cured at the deposition—such as objections to the form of the question (e.g., vague, ambiguous, compound questions, leading)—are reserved until trial and therefore need not be made at the deposition. Reserved objections will only be ruled upon if a party tries to use the response to the objectionable question at trial or at summary judgment. By contrast, objections going to the form of the question will be waived if not made during the deposition.

▼ Unless the objection is based on a privilege and there is an instruction not to answer, the deponent must answer the question, notwithstanding the objection.

▼ When opposing counsel makes improper objections, remind them of the rules, state your reliance on those rules for the record, and instruct the witness to answer the question without regard to the attorney's objection.

▼ After you have put your legal position on the record, you should stop arguing. Otherwise, if the dispute reaches the court, the court will see a transcript with both counsel behaving improperly and is likely to lay some of the blame for the dispute on you.

14. *Dealing with "speaking objections."* Speaking objections are objections that are suggestive or educational to the witness, such as "Objection, you are asking this witness to speculate on something she knows nothing about." Generally, the witness will then respond "I don't know." Another example is "Objection, the witness already testified that the light was green when she entered the intersection." The witness will then state that the light was green when she entered the intersection. Note your objection to the use of speaking objections on the record, and remind opposing counsel that they are only permitted to state the objection succinctly and should not coach the witness.

15. *Using exhibits.*

▼ Because all objections, other than those of form, are preserved, you need not establish an evidentiary foundation (e.g., the exhibit is authentic) before using an exhibit in a deposition. However, if you expect to use a document from a deposition to support a summary judgment motion, you must establish the evidentiary foundation for that document, because evidence relied upon at summary judgment must be admissible.

▼ For each document you plan to use as an exhibit in a deposition, you should have one copy for each counsel attending the deposition and one for yourself. The "original" copy of the exhibit will be marked by the court reporter (see below), used by witness during the deposition and preserved with the transcript after the deposition.

▼ Exhibits used in a deposition should be marked for identification purposes. The court reporter will mark each exhibit with a number, the date, and the name of the witness, and can do so without going off the record. However, the court reporter cannot mark an exhibit and transcribe any statements or questions by you at the same time. As you hand the document to the reporter and ask him or her to mark it, provide opposing counsel with a copy. After the court reporter has marked the exhibit, identify it on the record. For example, you can say "The court reporter has marked as *Exhibit 1,* for purposes of identification, a November 14, 2000, memorandum from Marley Johnson to Jasper Parr, with the 'Bates' number ABC0012-ABC0015."

▼ When there are multiple depositions in a case, it is helpful to continue the exhibit numbering sequence from deposition to deposition so that there will not be multiple documents marked "Exhibit 1" in the same case. As an alternative, each exhibit could be identified by witness, e.g., "Doherty Exhibit 1."

▼ When handing a witness a document or when referring to it on the record, always refer to it by exhibit number. Never say "this document." Similarly, if the deponent refers to "this document" during his testimony, clarify which document he is referring to by saying "When you say 'this document,' you mean Exhibit 1?" If you do not specifically identify a document referenced during a deposition, you will have an unclear record and, thus, a less useful one.

16. *Dealing with the difficult witness.* Witnesses often respond to questions but do not answer them. For example, a witness may not want to answer your question and, instead, will provide a colloquy that has little or nothing to do with your question.

▼ Do not be intimidated; appear confident.

▼ If you think a witness did not answer your question, ask the stenographer to read back your question and the witness' answer.

▼ Move to strike the non-responsive answer to preserve your position for trial.

▼ Ask the same question again. If the witness still does not answer the question, simply ask the stenographer to repeat your question. Repeat until you get your answer. This is a subtle but effective method of reminding the witness that her testimony is being recorded and demonstrating that her attempt to avoid the question is obvious.

▼ Alternatively, you can subtly embarrass the witness by offering to simplify the question for her. Then phrase the question as a true-false question.

▼ If all this fails, you may inform the witness that, at the end of her deposition, you will suspend the question, take the issue to the judge, and then come back and re-depose her, seeking all costs (including attorneys' fees) caused by her refusal to answer.

17 *Concluding a deposition.* At the end of a deposition, the questioning attorney should solidify the record by stating the following:

▼ Have you understood all the questions you answered?

▼ Did you answer my questions truthfully and fully?

▼ Is there any testimony that you have given today that you would like to change or supplement?

▶ Only if the questioning attorney has received all the discovery responses due at the time of the deposition and the witness has answered all questions asked should that attorney state that the deposition is "concluded." Otherwise, he should "adjourn" the deposition. If you are defending the deposition, you likely should object to these wrap-up questions, noting that the witness has responded to the questioning attorney's questions as best she understood them, based on her best recollection and memory at the time of the deposition.

CHAPTER 6

Legal Research

Yes, you wrote research memos in law school, but only you were affected by the grade you received on them. When you conduct research in a law firm, the assigning attorney and the client rely on you to provide the right answer and the client pays for your time. You also will discover very quickly that practicing lawyers are less available than law professors and much less tolerant of mistakes.

A research assignment may come to you from a senior partner who explains to you all the facts and the issue to be researched (along with some cool war stories), or it could come by phone from a stressed-out fifth-year associate at 11 p.m. In either case, the essence of the question will be the same: "Here are the facts—how does the law treat them?"

THINGS TO ASK WHEN YOU ARE ASSIGNED A RESEARCH PROJECT

1. *Preliminary questions.* Anytime you are asked to research a legal issue, ask the following:

   ▼ When does the assigning attorney need your work (i.e., what is the deadline for an answer)?

   ▼ Does the assignor need a written or oral answer? If written, see "Special Issues for Written Memos" below. If you are assigned an oral report, draft a mini-memo for yourself, noting the facts and holdings of the important cases you found. This will refresh your memory if your oral presentation is delayed or if you are later asked to provide a written memo.

   ▼ If you are writing a memo, to whom should it be addressed? The attorney? The client?

   ▼ Are there any special cost sensitivities?

   ▼ Are there sources of law or commentary that the assignor prefers?

2. *Substantive questions.* There are three substantive areas you must discuss with the assigning attorney before you begin the assignment:

   1) **Jurisdiction and Forum**

   ▼ Is the issue already in litigation? If so, where is it pending?

   ▼ If the issue is not yet in litigation, are certain forums better for your client?

   ▼ What body of law applies to the issue? State or federal? If state law, which state? If the assigning attorney does not know, this will be your first issue to research.

   ▼ If jurisdiction is an issue, ask where people and entities are domiciled, where events occurred, whether there are choice of law clauses involved, etc.

   2) **Legal Question**

   ▼ Understand the precise legal issue you are being asked to research. Can you reduce it to a simple question? After you receive an assignment, repeat back the one-sentence issue to the assigning attorney to make sure you understand exactly what you are asked to research.

   ▼ Your research may reveal that the issue needs to be clarified. If this happens, explain what you found, ask for clarification, and ask how the assigning attorney would like to proceed.

   3) **Facts**

   ▼ Make sure you know the names (and spellings) of people and/or entities involved, and understand the role of each. Know the timeline also. Often, it is helpful to draft a timeline to keep track of the order of events.

3. *Research in an effective, cost-conscious manner.* Good research is vital to good representation, but it is potentially very expensive for clients. Managing client costs will show you to have good judgment and professional maturity.

   ▼ Online research can be a very useful tool, but it also can be expensive. Understand how online research will be charged to the client and how to use it to maximize efficiency and cost effectiveness.

   ▼ Spend a few minutes formulating a query for an online search before you perform it.

   ▼ Understand how the online databases in which you perform a search are organized so you know your search is comprehensive but not excessive.

▼ Before using one of the major online databases, get the toll-free number for their research lawyers. Talk through your issue with them and ask them for help. This service is free and saves research time and money.

▼ When researching, take notes on the computer so you can easily copy any findings into a memo or brief. When reading cases, record information as follows:

1) *The facts.* Note the facts of the case and analyze the ways in which those facts are similar to, and different from, the facts of your case. Also note the procedural posture of the case.

2) *The issue decided.* Most likely, you will not find a case addressing precisely the same issue you are researching. The important thing is to find the most relevant analogs.

3) *The holding.* Make sure that you have separated the holding from dicta (conclusion not necessary to the court's decision). Dicta have less authority than holdings.

4) *The reasoning.* The court's reasoning will assist you in applying the holding of an analogous case.

4. *Organize the legal memorandum.*

▼ Law firm lawyers, like law professors, want your work presented in a format familiar to them.

▼ Ask the assigning attorney for the format he likes. You may also want to ask others for memos that they have prepared for the same lawyer. Also check to see if your firm has a standard format for memos.

▼ Practicing attorneys are busier than professors. They want an answer to the question earlier and more succinctly than professors. Put the answer early in the memo, such as in the "summary" or "short answer" sections, and let the rest of the memo provide more detail if they want it. Never save the answer for the conclusion at the end of the memo, although you may repeat it there.

If you do not receive guidance from the assigning lawyer on the format for the memo, use the one you were taught in law school:

1) **Statement of Facts.** Provide all relevant, known facts, whether they are good or bad for your client. Also identify any facts that are not known but which would impact your analysis.

2) **Question Presented.** State concisely the precise legal issue addressed by the memo. Phrase it as a question.

3) **Short Answer.** Answer the Question Presented, ideally in one sentence. The answer should never be longer than half a page.

    4) **Analysis.** Break the issue down into parts and subparts, and apply the governing law to the facts pertinent to each part and subpart. Where there is a statute or multi-part test from a case, address each element of it. Write objectively and anticipate and address the arguments of the adverse parties.

    5) **Conclusion.** Summarize the analysis in one or two paragraphs.

5. *Recheck your authorities: Are they still good law?* To ensure this:

▼ Run your cases through Shepard's or Key Cite. These resources, which you can find in the major online legal research databases, will tell you if the case has been overruled, superceded by statute, criticized, or otherwise cited by other decisions. If a particular holding in a case has been overruled or superceded by statute, it is no longer good law and should not be cited in support of that proposition. Note, however, that the fact that one proposition in a case has been overruled does not necessarily render the case useless; there may be other holdings in the case that survive. For this reason, you should always carefully review any case that may potentially overrule your case.

▼ Read advance sheets and legal newspapers for cases related to the issues you are researching.

▼ If the area of law is evolving, send an e-mail to other attorneys in your group, asking if they know of any new cases in the area of your research.

SPECIAL ISSUES FOR WRITTEN MEMOS

Ask about the depth of coverage desired and the expected length. Does the attorney want a short memorandum, covering only the basics? Does she want a lengthy, multi-jurisdictional analysis of a legal issue? Unless otherwise instructed by the assigning attorney, write legal research memoranda objectively and explore the strengths and weaknesses of all parties' positions on the issue. Write the memo so that someone with no knowledge of the facts or law can follow the analysis and the process by which you arrive at the conclusion.

Before you begin to draft the memo, provide the assigning attorney with a preview of your findings. Meet with the assigning attorney (or send her an e-mail or voicemail) telling her what your research indicates. This will help set her expectations and ensure that your memo does not miss any of the issues important to the assignor. It also gives her another opportunity to shape your research.

STYLE ISSUES

▶ Does your firm use special forms or computer macros for memos, such as special letterhead with "Attorney-Client Privilege/Work Product" on it?

▶ Err on the more formal side. Address the memo to "Charles B. Smart," not "Chuck Smart," even if he is addressed that way.

▶ What is the assigning lawyer's preference for spacing? Single? Double? What is his or her preference for indenting and justification?

BEFORE GIVING YOUR MEMO TO THE ASSIGNING ATTORNEY

▶ *Run spell check.* Surprisingly often, people fail to do this.

▶ *Proofread.* Typos will make you look careless, so do your best to minimize them. Some suggestions:

▼ Put the document away for a while and come back to it.

▼ Read the document from the back to the front.

▼ Read slowly with a ruler so that you can focus on each line.

▼ Ask your assistant or secretary to give the memo a final proofread.

▶ *Blue book.* Make sure that citations are in the correct form for memoranda.

▶ *Recheck your authorities.* Are they still good law?

CHAPTER 7

Motion Practice

GENERAL

A motion is a request that a court rule on an issue. Motions must persuade the court that one side of an argument is the right one.

The timing for filing a motion can be critical. For example, if a motion relates to discovery, you must file it while there is still time to conduct the discovery you seek (unless you plan to file a subsequent motion seeking to extend the discovery deadline).

Always consult the local rules of the court in which you will file a motion. They often impose prerequisites to filing a motion.

The rules generally require that motions be made in writing. A motion should:

1. Give notice to all parties;

2. State the specific relief sought; and

3. Argue the legal and factual basis for the relief sought. This argument is found in a "Memorandum of Points and Authorities" attached to the motion.

Memorandum of Points and Authorities

This memorandum gives the background of the dispute and argues for the relief requested. It should be written so that a judge with limited knowledge of the case can follow it easily. Memos of points and authority often are organized into three sections:

▶ *Background.* This provides the court with the factual background of the case and the issues relevant to the motion. Facts can be organized chronologically or by issue. Some attorneys think that presentation of the facts is the most persuasive aspect of the memo. Still, take care not to overstate the facts.

▶ *Argument.* This presents the law, applies it to the facts, and persuades the court to rule in the movant's favor. Cite authorities with the most precedential value, usually higher courts in the same jurisdiction. Avoid overstatements. Unless required by ethical standards, generally you should not raise legal authorities you expect the opposing party to use in support of their arguments, particularly if you are permitted to file a reply to the opposition's arguments. Doing so is distracting and defensive. But see Rule 11 of the Federal Rules for guidance on your ethical obligations.

▶ *Conclusion.* Succinctly restates the argument and requests that the motion be granted.

OTHER DOCUMENTS ATTACHED TO MOTIONS

PROPOSED ORDERS

Some courts require the submission of a proposed order. This is a draft of the order you wish the court to enter. Always consult local rules and the judge's clerk to determine if one is required or permitted.

AFFIDAVITS AND DECLARATIONS

Affidavits and declarations provide the means of putting evidence in support of a motion before the court. Both affidavits and declarations are sworn statements of fact. Affidavits are sworn before an authorized person (e.g., a notary); declarations are not. Affidavits and declarations should lay out each of the facts to which the affiant or declarant will swear in separate paragraphs and should state that the affiant/declarant has personal knowledge of the facts asserted in the affidavit and swears under the penalty of perjury that the contents are true and correct. The affidavit/declaration then can be cited in support of factual statements made in the motion. For example, if a declarant states that the traffic light was green when she entered the intersection, the motion itself can state that the light was green and cite the declaration.

Make sure to check local rules and statutes, such as Title 28 of the U.S. Code, for required language in any affidavit or declaration to be filed with a court and instances in which an affidavit or declaration must be submitted.

All motions and supporting papers should be served on all parties to an action.

CERTIFICATE OF SERVICE

Attach a Certificate of Service stating that the documents were served. A sample Certificate of Service is attached as Exhibit F. ━●

OPPOSING MEMORANDA AND REPLIES

If a motion is filed against your client, you will submit an opposing memorandum; if you fail to do so, you may concede the motion. An opposing memorandum should respond to the motion and demonstrate that the movant is not entitled to the relief it requests. Opposing memoranda contain counterstatements of the facts and legal analysis.

Some of the most common motions—Motions to Dismiss, Motions for Summary Judgment, and Motions to Compel—are discussed below.

MOTIONS TO DISMISS

A Motion to Dismiss for failure to state a claim (a "12(b)(6) motion" under the Federal Rules) asserts that, even if all facts asserted in a complaint are true, the complaint does not state a claim for which legal relief can be granted. This motion must be made in the first responsive pleading to the complaint (i.e., before the answer is filed). The party moving to dismiss must demonstrate that the claimant has not sufficiently alleged facts that would entitle it to relief. In deciding a Motion to Dismiss, courts are limited to the facts alleged in the pleadings, undisputed documents incorporated in the pleadings (such as a contract appended to a complaint), and matters of which the court may take judicial notice (such as public records).

TIPS AND SUGGESTIONS

1. *Evaluate every claim for its Motion to Dismiss potential.* Do the allegations of the complaint establish each element of the claimant's claim? Do those allegations reveal a legal basis for dismissing the claim (such as the expiration of the statute of limitations)? Common reasons for filing a Motion to Dismiss include the following:

   ▼ Failure to plead facts supporting each element of the claim: For example, a fraud claim that fails to plead the claimant's reliance on the alleged fraud should be dismissed.

   ▼ Novel legal theory: Attempts to create new causes of action are proper subjects for Motions to Dismiss.

   ▼ Educate the judge: Motions to Dismiss can be used to educate the judge about the weakness of the claimant's case.

2. *Include all the right documents.* Under the local rules of most federal courts and many state courts, a motion must include a separate memorandum of law that provides the legal argument for the motion.

3. *Do not miss deadlines.* A Motion to Dismiss must be made in the first pleading that responds to the claim and within a number of days set by local rules. If you lose the Motion to Dismiss, the Federal Rules require that you answer the complaint within ten days of the court's ruling.

4. *Draft professionally.* All motions should effectively convey your client's story, but, as with other filed documents, you are drafting a public document with your client's and firm's names on it. The same reporters who cover the courts and read complaints also read motions. Thus, do not write anything in a motion that would make you, your client, or your firm uncomfortable if it appeared in the morning newspaper. Some issues to consider (and discuss with your assigning attorney) regarding the motion:

   ▼ Ask the assigning attorney for an example of a prior motion that he liked. This example should tell you the tone preferred by the assigning lawyer.

   ▼ Do not assume that a reader of the motion will have any familiarity with the facts or with any party to the case. As with complaints, consider including facts that make an implicit point for your client.

   ▼ Do not include extraneous language or artificial formality; write short, clear sentences with the same formality you would use in normal business correspondence.

   ▼ Do not use invective or melodrama in motions. This language makes the motion less persuasive.

   ▼ Avoid legalisms such as "heretofore" and the like.

   ▼ Avoid sarcasm and attempts at humor.

   ▼ Use good judgment in how you reflect your client's view of the opposing party.

   ▼ Do not assume any subject-specific sophistication by the court; explain all of the facts in plain English.

5. *Prepare the client for a loss.* Make sure that your client understands that Motions to Dismiss can be long-shots, particularly in state courts.

   A sample Motion to Dismiss is attached as Exhibit K-1 and a sample Memorandum of Points and Authorities supporting the motion is attached as Exhibit K-2. ➙

SUMMARY JUDGMENT MOTIONS

A Motion for Summary Judgment seeks a ruling on a claim or claims before trial on the grounds that there is no dispute as to a material fact and the moving party is entitled to judgment as a matter of law. A disputed material fact will prevent entry of summary judgment, but a dispute over a legal issue will not. In opposing a Motion for Summary Judgment, the respondent should establish a dispute as to a material fact.

Most courts require that the party moving for summary judgment submit a separate document identifying all undisputed material facts necessary to its motion, usually called a Statement of Undisputed Material Facts (a sample of which is attached as Exhibit L). The Statement of Undisputed Material Facts lays out the material facts you allege to be true in support of your motion. For each fact you must cite the evidence supporting it, such as deposition testimony, an affidavit, or a response to an interrogatory. The evidence cited in the Statement of Undisputed Material Facts should be attached to the Statement itself when it is submitted to the court.

TIPS AND SUGGESTIONS

1. *Make an early assessment of the potential for a summary judgment motion.* At the beginning of a case, determine whether any claims can be resolved with a summary judgment motion. Your proof plan should indicate whether you will have the evidence you need to make or refute each claim prior to trial, and whether there are disputed factual issues.

2. *Confirm that you have admissible evidence supporting the claim(s) on which you are moving for summary judgment.* Do not file a motion for summary judgment if you do not have admissible evidence that supports each of the claims on which the motion is based. Likewise, if you expect to be defending against a motion for summary judgment, determine what evidence you will need to demonstrate that the facts the moving party must show to obtain summary judgment are disputed.

3. *Set forth the undisputed facts in a clear manner.* As discussed above, many jurisdictions require a separate document that sets forth each undisputed fact that supports the motion in separate numbered paragraphs. These jurisdictions also require that movants identify the evidence that establishes each of those facts. The document identifying the facts is called a Statement of Undisputed Material Facts. Even if your jurisdiction does not require it, preparing one is a good practice.

4. *Attach the documents that support the motion.* File with the motion all documents—Statement of Undisputed Material Facts (if required) and affidavits, deposition excerpts, exhibits, discovery responses, etc.—on which the motion relies. In addition, the local rules of most federal courts and many state courts require that a motion include a separate Memorandum of Points and Authorities that provides the legal argument. Do not forget to attach a Certificate of Service.

5. *Do not create any issues of fact, even if the facts are immaterial.* Parties opposing a Motion for Summary Judgment often will try to bait the moving party by raising, in its opposition, a fact that it knows the moving party disputes. Do not take the bait. Do not even dispute the fact in a footnote while noting that it is not material.

6. *Draft professionally.* All motions should effectively convey your client's story, but, as with other filed documents, you are drafting a public document with your client's and firm's names on it. The same reporters who cover the courts and read complaints also read motions. Thus, do not write anything in a motion that would make you, your firm, or your client uncomfortable if it appeared in the morning newspaper. Some issues to consider (and discuss with your assigning attorney) regarding the motion:

▼ Ask the assigning attorney for an example of a prior motion that he liked. This example should tell you the tone preferred by the assigning lawyer.

▼ Do not assume that a reader of the motion will have any familiarity with the facts or with any party to the case. As with complaints, consider including facts that make an implicit point for your client.

▼ Do not include extraneous language or artificial formality; write short, clear sentences with the same formality you would use in normal business correspondence.

▼ Do not use invective or melodrama in motions. This language makes the motion less persuasive.

▼ Avoid legalisms such as "heretofore" and the like.

▼ Avoid sarcasm and attempts at humor.

▼ Use good judgment in how you reflect your client's view of the opposing party.

▼ Do not assume any subject-specific sophistication by the court; explain all of the facts in plain English.

A sample Motion for Summary Judgment is attached as Exhibit M-1 and a sample Memorandum of Points and Authorities supporting the motion is attached as Exhibit M-2. ➙

MOTION TO COMPEL DISCOVERY

A party may file a motion seeking an order that the opposing party respond to its discovery requests. Motions to compel are useful to force another party to:

► Provide Initial Disclosures;

► Answer a question asked at a deposition;

▶ Designate an appropriate person to testify on behalf of an entity in a deposition (such as a deposition under Rule 30(b)(6) of the Federal Rules);

▶ Respond fully to an interrogatory or request for production; or

▶ Provide a log of documents and information withheld on the grounds of privilege.

NOTE: Prior to filing a Motion to Compel Discovery, the Federal Rules (and many state rules) require that the moving party attempt to confer with the adverse party to obtain the contested discovery or to narrow the areas of disagreement. The motion must contain a certification that such efforts were made. A party against whom a Motion to Compel is filed may respond by opposing the motion and by filing a cross-motion for a protective order to prevent discovery of the contested issue. A court may award the costs associated with a Motion to Compel, including attorneys fees, to the prevailing party.

TIPS AND SUGGESTIONS

1. *Respond to a failure to provide discovery immediately.* A discovery dispute might arise where the party requesting material does not believe it has received an adequate response. You may be able to diffuse a discovery dispute and protect your client as follows:

   ▼ As soon as an opposing party has failed to provide discovery or has provided responses you believe to be inadequate, arrange a telephone conference with opposing counsel to discuss your concerns.

   ▼ If the opposing party agrees to provide the requested discovery, be sure to set a deadline.

   ▼ Follow this conversation with a letter documenting your concerns and the response of the opposing party and/or counsel, including the agreed deadline.

   ▼ If the opposing party still does not cure the deficiencies of its discovery responses, arrange another meeting and advise counsel that you intend to file a Motion to Compel Discovery if the deficiencies are not corrected.

   ▼ Again, this meeting should be followed by a letter documenting what occurred and any agreed deadline.

2. *Establish your good faith efforts to resolve the dispute.* Attach to your declaration in support of your Motion to Compel, your discovery requests, your letters related to discovery, and the response of opposing counsel.

3. *Include all the right documents.* Under the local rules of most federal courts and many state courts, a Motion to Compel Discovery must include a certification of the efforts made to resolve the dispute and a separate Memorandum of Points and Authorities that provides the legal argument for the motion. Check the local rules for additional requirements and include a Certificate of Service with your motion.

A sample Motion to Compel Discovery is attached as Exhibit N-1 and a sample Memorandum of Points and Authorities supporting the motion is attached as Exhibit N-2. ••

CHAPTER 8

Settlement and Dismissal

Settlement, negotiation, and alternative dispute resolution are beyond the scope of this book. But this section provides some guidance on settlement agreements because junior associates are sometimes asked to draft them.

The settlement agreement is a contract that ends the litigation of the issues described in the agreement for the people named in the agreement. It includes a "release of claims" in exchange for agreed upon consideration (which may be money or something else). Counsel for both sides usually negotiate for the right to create the first draft so that they can frame the issues and agreement in a manner most beneficial to their client. The form of settlement agreements varies widely depending upon the facts of the specific case.

TIPS AND SUGGESTIONS

1. *Do not reinvent the wheel.* Get a sample settlement agreement from the assigning attorney. But make sure that you carefully review all aspects of your draft with the specifics of your dispute in mind. Also be sure to compare the breadth of the release from the sample with that of the intended release in your case: should they be the same or is one intended to be a broader release than the other?

2. *Identify the parties comprehensively.* The agreement should broadly describe the parties released from claims and the parties precluded from making claims as well. Make sure to include all affiliates, partners, successors, related entities, and the like.

3. *There are two types of releases: general releases and limited releases.* A general release wipes the slate clean by releasing any and all claims between the parties, whether or not those claims were raised in the litigation or dispute that is being settled. A limited release releases the parties from claims arising out of specifically identified facts and circumstances identified in the release; other claims remain viable.

▼ If you are drafting a limited release, identify the disputed issues carefully. Take great care in describing the issues underlying the legal dispute (not merely the legal claims). The released party benefits from a broad description of the issue, while the interest of the releasing party is served by a narrower one.

▼ If you are drafting a general release, make sure you understand whether there is any remaining business relationship or obligations between the parties. If there is, you may want to use a limited release or "carve out" rights and claims related to the ongoing relationship or obligations from the release.

4. *List the actions barred by the release.* The current suit must cease as a consequence of the release, as well as other potential actions, such as demands, contribution, indemnity, etc.

5. *Identify the court* and/or other proceedings that are pending between the parties and how the parties have agreed to end them.

6. *Identify the terms of the settlement.* Describe precisely what payment and/or conduct is expected in return for the claims released.

7. *Consider whether your client would like the agreement to be confidential.* If you cannot determine their view on this, assume they would. Insert broad mutual confidentiality language into the agreement.

8. *Consider requiring each party to agree to refrain from disparaging the other.*

9. *If an employee is involved, consult a labor lawyer.* There are laws applicable to the settlement of some employer-employee claims. Violating these can cause the settlement agreement to be voided. Similarly, if the settlement involves a large payment to your client, consider consulting a tax attorney who can advise the client on the appropriate tax treatment of the settlement.

10. *Include language that says the settlement does not constitute an admission of liability on the part of either party.*

11. *Include standard miscellaneous contractual terms.* For example, include a choice of law and forum selection provisions to govern the dispute in the event that either party breaches it. Also, it is advisable to include provisions allowing signature in counterparts, precluding oral modifications and stating that the present agreement is integrated and supercedes prior ones.

12. *Research the legal requirements of settlement agreement and release under the applicable law.* Some states void releases which fail to include mandated statutory language or which attempt to contract around the language.

Once the settlement agreement has been executed, the case should be dismissed. Under the Federal Rules, a plaintiff may voluntarily dismiss (withdraw) its case either with or without prejudice. If the case is dismissed without prejudice, the claims may be re-filed at a later time. If a case is dismissed with prejudice, the plaintiff cannot pursue any of those claims in the future. Unless stated otherwise, a voluntary dismissal by stipulation will be deemed to be without prejudice. Accordingly, if your settlement provides for dismissal with prejudice, make sure the dismissal document filed in court so states.

There are three ways to voluntarily dismiss a case:

1. The plaintiff unilaterally files a Notice of Dismissal before the defendant files an answer or a Motion for Summary Judgment, whichever occurs first;

2. A stipulation signed by all parties to dismiss the action, which can be filed at any time; or

3. A motion seeking an order of voluntary dismissal if it is too late for a unilateral notice and some parties refuse to stipulate.

A sample Settlement Agreement is attached as Exhibit O-1 and a sample Notice of Dismissal is attached as Exhibit O-2. ➥

CHAPTER 9

Service of Process

Process is the means by which a court commands the served entity to appear somewhere. Service of process is used to gain jurisdiction over a person or entity in a lawsuit by serving that person or entity with the complaint and summons. Service of process is also used to require a non-party to litigation to appear for a deposition or to produce documents in connection with that litigation via a subpoena. "Service" is the actual or constructive delivery of the court's command (a summons or a subpoena) to a person or an entity.

Service of process requires personal delivery of the document to be served to the person or entity. Although process may be served by any non-party to the litigation over the age of 18, most attorneys use a professional (hired) process server.

The particular method by which process may be served varies by the type of person or entity to be served. Rules for serving process on corporations, associations, partnerships, domestic individuals, individuals in foreign countries, and infants or incompetent persons differ. The rules of the court in which the action is pending specify how process must be served on each kind of entity. If you fail to follow these rules precisely, you risk a court finding process to be invalid. If process is invalid, the court does not have jurisdiction over the person or entity and that person or entity is not required to appear or produce documents.

If you represent a defendant who has yet to be served with a complaint and summons, the plaintiff may ask if you will waive formal service of process on your client. Review the rules regarding service of process (and waiver) because there may be a *hidden trap*. For example, under the Federal Rules, a court may impose the costs of effecting service (including the costs of a motion seeking such costs) on defendants who fail to waive formal service and cannot establish good cause for the failure. Also, some courts' rules give defendants waiving service of process an extended time during which to respond to the complaint.

If you are assigned the task of serving a summons and complaint or a third-party subpoena:

► Get the name of a reliable process server (ask other attorneys or paralegals).

► If you expect any problem in service, warn the process server (even though service could cost more).

► Obtain checks for all fees that must be paid in connection with service of process. You will need to pay the process server for his or her services. If you are serving a subpoena for a nonparty to appear at a deposition, you must deliver a check for the nonparty's "witness fee" (which is provided in statutes and/or court rules).

► Review with the process server the law regarding the manner of service (how service should be made).

► Note in your calendar when you expect to hear that service was effected.

► Ask the process server to contact you when the document has been served and to provide you with the time and place it was served and the name of the person accepting service.

► The process server will sign an affidavit stating when and how service was made. Make sure the process server completes the affidavit promptly after service and sends it to you. Also, make sure the affidavit notes all documents that were served (such as a subpoena and a witness fee, or the complaint and a summons). The rules of some courts will require that you file the affidavit of service. In other cases, you will only need it if the person or entity served attempts to contest service.

► Be careful to note all local service rules, especially where service is made in an unfamiliar jurisdiction.

CHAPTER 10

Managing Exhibits at Trial

If you are lucky, the senior attorney on a case with you will ask a paralegal with trial experience to manage exhibits at trial, thereby taking those duties off your plate and giving you more time for a substantive role in the trial. Managing exhibits at trial is extremely important and can be an enormous task, even in a case that is not document-intensive. If you have other substantive roles in the trial, it will be challenging for you to manage the documents at the same time are performing these other duties.

The best way to learn how to manage exhibits at trial is to observe the process. In the absence of that opportunity, take a few hours to speak with someone who has previously managed exhibits during a trial.

▶ In general, you need copies of the following documents at trial:

1. All pleadings.
2. Discovery requests and responses, and any correspondence related thereto.
3. Plaintiff's pre-marked exhibits.
4. Any orders or rulings by the court in the case.
5. All deposition transcripts.

You should keep these documents nearby and they should be easily accessible.

▶ Bring multiple copies of each exhibit that may be used in direct or cross-examination. In a bench trial, you will need one each for the judge, opposing counsel, the witness, and yourself. In a jury trial, you may need additional copies for the jury, depending on the judge's practice with respect to providing jurors with documents during trial, and depending on the use of blow-ups, overheads, etc. Make sure you understand all of the judge's rules on use of exhibits (and technology for displaying exhibits) well in advance of the trial.

▶ Sort the exhibits into sets by placing the copies of each exhibit in a folder. Then group sets of exhibits together by the witness with whom you expect them to be used. Keep the folders of each exhibit in the order in which you expect them to be used.

▶ Also, have a list of each party's exhibits with columns in which to note whether the exhibit has been admitted or ruled inadmissible along with related information (e.g., "Court declined to admit pending foundation from Witness X").

▶ Finally, always talk to the senior attorney on the case for her advice. She may have a certain way she likes the documents organized. Also get the advice of attorneys and assistants who have tried cases with her before.

OTHER ROLES AT TRIAL

If you are playing a substantive role in the trial, you may be examining and cross-examining witnesses. You may also be asked to make the opening statement or the closing argument. The substantive tasks you will be asked to perform often depend upon your firm's practices; as a general proposition, new and junior associates in smaller law firms are more likely to perform more substantive roles at trial (and get more trial experience). Regardless of the size of your firm, however, you should be ready to dive in, if asked. Detailed advice for trial practice is beyond the scope of this book, but there are a few things you can do to prepare yourself for when the opportunity arises:

▶ Look for and take opportunities to observe trials of senior lawyers. You will learn an enormous amount about trials just by watching. You also show interest in developing your skills, which will make a great impression on those senior lawyers. It may lead them to come to you the next time they are looking for an associate to add to their trial team.

▶ Participate in any training your firm offers. Again, you likely will learn a lot and will make a great impression on the senior lawyers conducting the training.

▶ Attend trial work courses offered by outside organizations (such as bar associations and professional legal training organizations). Even if you have a good in-house training program, it is good to see other approaches and styles.

▶ Never pass up opportunities to conduct depositions. Depositions practice is related to direct and cross-examination practice. You will gain valuable experience in dealing with witnesses in depositions. Deposition experience also will boost your confidence in your ability to deal with witnesses during a trial.

▶ Know the applicable rules of evidence cold. Even if you had a good evidence class in law school, you may want to take a refresher course from an organization that offers legal training for lawyers.

CHAPTER 11

Survival in Court

SOME BASIC GUIDELINES FOR YOUR FIRST COURT APPEARANCE

▶ Your appearance reflects on your firm and your client, so make sure your attire is appropriate, respectful, and serious. There is no casual day in court. Some lawyers are famous for flashy clothes. Until you are famous (hopefully for something else), do not copy them.

▶ Before the day of your court appearance, make sure you know the location of the courthouse and have directions to it and to the courtroom where you must appear. If you have any doubt about the location of the courthouse or how long it will take you to get there, do a "dry run" and time the trip. This is particularly a good idea if you will be traveling to the court during rush hour and you do not know how much that will lengthen your travel time.

▶ When you arrive in the courtroom, introduce yourself to the court reporter and the judge's clerk. You also should introduce yourself to opposing counsel if you have not met him before, or greet him if you have.

▶ In the unlikely event that the judge is sitting at the bench before your opposing counsel arrives, you should not make idle chitchat with the judge; this may be considered *ex parte* contact and, in most cases, is not allowed.

▶ When the judge enters the courtroom, you should stand up, as you will be instructed to do, and you should not sit down until directed to do so. Whenever you address the judge, you should stand—even if to answer a question from the judge with a one-word response. Similarly, always address the judge as "Judge Doherty" or "Your Honor," never "sir" or "ma'am" (as in "yes, sir" or "yes, ma'am"). Some female judges, in particular, are sensitive to being referred to as "ma'am" instead of "Your Honor."

▶ When you appear before the court, bring a few extra copies of any documents that may be discussed. You may need the copies if the judge does not have a copy of the documents in front of him or if the court reporter needs a copy to assist with the transcript. If you previously submitted a proposed order on the motion to the court, you should bring a extra copy of that order. That way, if the judge states that she will grant your motion, you can hand up your proposed order and get it signed by the judge right away.

▶ If you are asked or given permission to hand a document to the judge, you should show it to opposing counsel and then hand it to the judge's clerk (unless the judge directs otherwise).

▶ No matter what the relationship between you and the opposing lawyer, or your client and the opposing lawyer's client, treat them cordially and professionally in (and out of) court.

Sample "Barebones" Complaint

UNITED STATES DISTRICT COURT FOR

THE SOUTHERN DISTRICT OF SURVIVAL[1]

OLIVIA KENSINGTON,	)	
[Address]	)	
Plaintiff,	)	
v.	)	Case No. 02-0001
OLIVER GORDON,	)	
[Address]	)	
Defendant.	)	
	)	

COMPLAINT

Plaintiff Olivia Kensington alleges against defendant Oliver Gordon as follows:

INTRODUCTION[2]

1. Ms. Kensington brings this action against Mr. Gordon to recover for his breach of contract. As a result of Mr. Gordon's breach of contract, Ms. Kensington has suffered losses in excess of eighty thousand dollars ($80,000).

---

[1] The heading of a complaint must provide the name of the court, the parties and title of the action (e.g., A, plaintiff v. D, defendant), the case number and the nature of the pleading (e.g., Complaint). Fed. R. Civ. P. 10(a). In addition, the parties' addresses must be stated in the caption of the complaint. The format and style of captions vary across jurisdictions. You should, therefore, review the requirements of the court's local rules and the common practice in that jurisdiction.

[2] A very brief introduction can orient the reader to the plaintiff's story, but it is not required under the Federal Rules. Nonetheless, an introduction is helpful to the reader and is, therefore, recommended.

JURISDICTION AND PARTIES[3]

2. The jurisdiction of this court is based on diversity of citizenship under 28 U.S.C. § 1332.
3. Ms. Kensington is a citizen of the State of Georgia and Mr. Gordon is a citizen of the state of Maryland. The matter in controversy exceeds the sum of seventy-five thousand dollars ($75,000), exclusive of interest and costs.

VENUE[4]

4. Venue is proper under 28 U.S.C. § 1391 because a substantial part of the events and omissions giving rise to this case occurred in this district.

FACTS[5]

5. On or about June 22, 2002, Ms. Kensington and Mr. Gordon entered into a contract for the purchase of one million (1,000,000) tennis balls. A true and correct copy of this contract is attached as Exhibit 1.
6. Pursuant to the contract, Ms. Kensington tendered to Mr. Gordon the sum of eighty thousand dollars ($80,000) on September 30, 2002, as payment for the tennis balls to be delivered under the contract on or before October 20, 2002.
7. Mr. Gordon failed and/or refused to deliver the tennis balls to Ms. Kensington on October 20, 2002.
8. Mr. Gordon has failed and/or refused to deliver the tennis balls to Ms. Kensington after October 20, 2002.

COUNT I—BREACH OF CONTRACT[6]

9. Ms. Kensington hereby incorporations by reference the allegations of paragraphs 1–8 as if fully set forth herein.[7]
10. Ms. Kensington and Mr. Gordon are parties to a valid, binding, and enforceable contract, pursuant to which Mr. Gordon agreed to deliver to Ms. Kensington one million (1,000,000) tennis balls for a fee of eighty thousand dollars ($80,000).

---

[3] Fed. R. Civ. P. 8(a)(1) requires that a complaint state the basis for the court's jurisdiction over it. A complaint that fails to allege the legal and factual bases for the court's jurisdiction may be subject to dismissal.

[4] Allegations supporting the venue of the case are not required, but, because improper venue is an affirmative defense and the court may want to be assured that venue is proper at the outset, the plaintiff should plead the legal and factual basis for it.

[5] The allegations set forth in the facts section should tell the plaintiff's story in narrative fashion, in numbered paragraphs. The facts section should read like a narrative—i.e., tell a story—and facts supporting the plaintiff's claims should be pled together in the facts section, rather than claim by claim. If there is more than one Count in the complaint, the facts should be titled "Facts Common to All Counts."

[6] Fed. R. Civ. P. 10(b) requires that the plaintiff state each claim separately. If there are multiple defendants and some claims apply to more than one defendant, the claims against each defendant should be stated separately. Thus, if the plaintiff alleges a claim for breach of contract against Defendant A and Defendant B, those claims should be stated in separate counts.

[7] Because the facts supporting all claims are alleged in the Facts section, the plaintiff need not repeat the specific facts supporting each cause of action in each Count.

11. Ms. Kensington performed all of her obligations under the contract.
12. Mr. Gordon breached his obligations under the contract, without justification or excuse, by failing to deliver to Ms. Kensington one million (1,000,000) tennis balls on or before October 20, 2002.
13. As a direct and proximate cause of Mr. Gordon's breach of the contract, Ms. Kensington has suffered damages in excess of eighty thousand dollars ($80,000) plus interest and costs.

WHEREFORE, plaintiff Ms. Kensington respectfully prays for judgment against defendant Mr. Gordon as follows:

1. For the sum of eighty thousand dollars ($80,000), plus interest and costs; and
2. For such other and further relief as the Court may deem proper.[8]

Jury trial demanded.[9]

Dated[10]
    [Name of attorney(s) of record]
    [Bar No., if required]
    [Firm]
    [Address]
    [Phone and fax numbers]

---

[8] A complaint must demand judgment and request relief. In a complaint containing multiple Counts, the plaintiff may demand judgment and request relief at the end of each Count, or at the end of the complaint itself. The plaintiff need not demand a specific amount of money, but if jurisdiction of the case is premised on diversity and a claim in over $75,000, the demand should state that the plaintiff seeks an amount in excess of $75,000.

[9] Under the Federal Rules, a plaintiff with a right to a jury trial need not demand a jury in the complaint. See Fed. R. Civ. P. 38(b). However, because the right to demand a jury trial may be waived if not timely asserted, it is advisable to include it in the complaint.

[10] The rules of the court in which the complaint is filed determine who may sign it. In general, only an attorney admitted to practice in a particular court may sign documents filed in that court. Further, even if authorized by the court's rules to sign pleading, junior associates should not presume that they will be signing them. It is advisable to check with the assigning attorney before signing any document to be filed with the court.

Sample Detailed Complaint

UNITED STATES DISTRICT COURT FOR

THE SOUTHERN DISTRICT OF SURVIVAL[1]

OLIVIA KENSINGTON,
[Address]
    Plaintiff,
       v.
OLIVER GORDON,
[Address]
    Defendant.
	)
	)
	)
	)
	)
	)
	)
	)
	)
		Case No. 02-0001

COMPLAINT

Plaintiff Olivia Kensington alleges against defendant Oliver Gordon as follows:

INTRODUCTION[2]

1. Ms. Kensington brings this action against Mr. Gordon to recover for his breach of contract. As a result of Mr. Gordon's breach of contract, Ms. Kensington has suffered losses in excess of eighty thousand dollars ($80,000).

---

[1] The heading of a complaint must provide the name of the court, the parties and title of the action (e.g., A, plaintiff v. D, defendant), the case number and the nature of the pleading (e.g., Complaint). Fed. R. Civ. P. 10(a). In addition, the parties' addresses must be stated in the caption of the complaint. The format and style of captions vary across jurisdictions. You should, therefore, review the requirements of the court's local rules and the common practice in that jurisdiction.

[2] A very brief introduction can orient the reader to the plaintiff's story, but it is not required under the Federal Rules. Nonetheless, an introduction is helpful to the reader and is, therefore, recommended.

JURISDICTION AND PARTIES[3]

2. The jurisdiction of this court is based on diversity of citizenship under 28 U.S.C. § 1332.
3. Ms. Kensington is a citizen of the State of Georgia and Mr. Gordon is a citizen of the state of Maryland. The matter in controversy exceeds the sum of seventy-five thousand dollars ($75,000), exclusive of interest and costs.

VENUE[4]

4. Venue is proper under 28 U.S.C. § 1391 because a substantial part of the events and omissions giving rise to this case occurred in this district.

FACTS[5]

5. On or about May 1, 2002, Ms. Kensington contacted Mr. Gordon regarding the purchase of tennis balls.
6. Following the May 1, 2002, meeting, Ms. Kensington and Mr. Gordon negotiated the terms and conditions of Ms. Kensington's purchase of tennis balls from Mr. Gordon.
7. Mr. Gordon offered to sell Ms. Kensington five hundred thousand (500,000) tennis balls at a per unit price of ten cents ($0.10) each.
8. Ms. Kensington rejected Mr. Gordon's offer to sell five hundred thousand (500,000) tennis balls for ten cents ($0.10) each.
9. Ms. Kensington then offered to purchase one million (1,000,000) tennis balls from Mr. Gordon for eight cents ($0.08) each.
10. Mr. Gordon accepted this offer.
11. On or about June 22, 2002, Ms. Kensington and Mr. Gordon entered into a contract for the purchase of one million (1,000,000) tennis balls at a per unit price of eight cents ($0.08). A true and correct copy of this contract is attached as Exhibit 1.
12. Pursuant to the contract, Ms. Kensington tendered to Mr. Gordon the sum of eighty thousand dollars ($80,000) on September 30, 2002, as payment for the tennis balls.
13. Pursuant to be delivered under the contract, Mr. Gordon was obligated to deliver the one million (1,000,000) tennis balls to Ms. Kensington on or before October 20, 2002.

---

[3] Fed. R. Civ. P. 8(a)(1) requires that a complaint state the basis for the court's jurisdiction over it. A complaint that fails to allege the legal and factual bases for the court's jurisdiction may be subject to dismissal.

[4] Allegations supporting the venue of the case are not required, but, because improper venue is an affirmative defense and the court may want to be assured that venue is proper at the outset, the plaintiff should plead the legal and factual basis for it.

[5] The allegations set forth in the facts section should tell the plaintiff's story in narrative fashion, in numbered paragraphs. The facts section should read like a narrative—i.e., tell a story—and facts supporting the plaintiff's claims should be pled together in the facts section, rather than claim by claim. If there is more than one Count in the complaint, the facts should be titled "Facts Common to All Counts."

14. Mr. Gordon failed to deliver the tennis balls to Ms. Kensington on or before October 20, 2002.
15. On or about October 23, 2002, Ms. Kensington contacted Mr. Gordon regarding delivery of the tennis balls.
16. During their conversation on October 23, 2002, Mr. Gordon admitted that he received payment for the tennis balls from Ms. Kensington and stated that the tennis balls were in transit and should be received on or before October 27, 2002.
17. As of October 29, Ms. Kensington had not received the tennis balls from Mr. Gordon, and she attempted to contact him again.
18. Since October 29, 2002, Mr. Gordon has not returned Ms. Kensington's calls, letters, and e-mail messages regarding delivery of the tennis balls.
19. Mr. Gordon has failed and/or refused to deliver the tennis balls to Ms. Kensington.

COUNT I—BREACH OF CONTRACT[6]

20. Ms. Kensington hereby incorporations by reference the allegations of paragraphs 1–19 as if fully set forth herein.[7]
21. Ms. Kensington and Mr. Gordon are parties to a valid, binding, and enforceable contract, pursuant to which Mr. Gordon agreed to deliver to Ms. Kensington one million (1,000,000) tennis balls for a fee of eighty thousand dollars ($80,000).
22. Ms. Kensington performed all of her obligations under the contract.
23. Mr. Gordon breached his obligations under the contract, without justification or excuse, by failing to deliver to Ms. Kensington one million (1,000,000) tennis balls on or before October 20, 2002.
24. As a direct and proximate cause of Mr. Gordon's breach of the contract, Ms. Kensington has suffered damages in excess of $80,000 plus interest and costs.

WHEREFORE, plaintiff Ms. Kensington respectfully prays for judgment against defendant Mr. Gordon as follows:

1. For the sum of eighty thousand dollars ($80,000), plus interest and costs; and
2. For such other and further relief as the Court may deem proper.[8]

---

[6] Fed. R. Civ. P. 10(b) requires that the plaintiff state each claim separately. If there are multiple defendants and some claims apply to more than one defendant, the claims against each defendant should be stated separately. Thus, if the plaintiff alleges a claim for breach of contract against Defendant A and Defendant B, those claims should be stated in separate counts.

[7] Because the facts supporting all claims are alleged in the facts section, the plaintiff need not repeat the specific facts supporting each cause of action in each Count. However, to ensure that all factual allegations that are necessary to support the cause of action of each Count are pled, a statement that the factual allegations are incorporated in the Count is necessary.

[8] A complaint must demand judgment and request relief. In a complaint containing multiple Counts, the plaintiff may demand judgment and request relief at the end of each Count, or at the end of the complaint itself. The plaintiff need not demand a specific amount of money, but if jurisdiction of the case is premised on diversity and a claim in over $75,000, the demand should state that the plaintiff seeks an amount in excess of $75,000.

Jury trial demanded.[9]

Dated[10]
    [Name of attorney(s) of record]
    [Bar No., if required]
    [Firm]
    [Address]
    [Phone and fax numbers]

---

[9] Under the Federal Rules, a plaintiff with a right to a jury trial need not demand a jury in the complaint. See Fed. R. Civ. P. 38(b). However, because the right to demand a jury trial may be waived if not timely asserted, it is advisable to include it in the complaint.

[10] The rules of the court in which the complaint is filed determine who may sign it. In general, only an attorney admitted to practice in a particular court may sign documents filed in that court. Further, even if authorized by the court's rules to sign pleading, junior associates should not presume that they will be signing them. It is advisable to check with the assigning attorney before signing any document to be filed with the court.

EXHIBIT C

Sample Answer

UNITED STATES DISTRICT COURT FOR

THE SOUTHERN DISTRICT OF SURVIVAL[1]

OLIVIA KENSINGTON,	)	
[Address]	)	
Plaintiff,	)	
v.	)	Case No. 02-0001
OLIVER GORDON,	)	JURY TRIAL
[Address]	)	DEMANDED
Defendant.	)	
	)	
	)	

ANSWER

Defendant Oliver Gordon, responds to the Complaint filed against him in this case and states as follows:

JURISDICTION

1. The allegations in paragraph 1 are legal conclusions to which no response is required. To the extent a response is required, Mr. Gordon denies the allegations and demands strict proof thereof.

---

[1] The heading of an answer must provide the name of the court, the parties and title of the action (e.g., A, plaintiff v. D, defendant), the case number and the nature of the pleading (e.g., Answer). Fed. R. Civ. P. 10(a). In addition, the parties' addresses must be stated in the caption of an answer. The format and style of captions vary across jurisdictions. You should, therefore, review the requirements of the court's local rules and the common practice in that jurisdiction.

2. Mr. Gordon admits that he is a citizen of the state of Maryland. Oliver is without sufficient information or knowledge to admit or deny all remaining allegations in paragraph 2 and therefore denies the allegations and demands strict proof thereof.

VENUE

3. The allegations in paragraph 1 are legal conclusions to which no response is required. To the extent a response is required, Mr. Gordon denies the allegations and demands strict proof thereof.

FACTS

4. Mr. Gordon denies the allegations of paragraph 4 and demands strict proof thereof. Mr. Gordon further denies that the document attached to the Complaint as Exhibit 1 constitutes a contract.
5. Mr. Gordon denies the allegations of paragraph 5 and demands strict proof thereof.
6. Mr. Gordon denies the allegations of paragraph 6 and demands strict proof thereof.
7. Mr. Gordon denies the allegations of paragraph 7 and demands strict proof thereof.

COUNT I—BREACH OF CONTRACT

8. Mr. Gordon hereby incorporates by reference the responses to the allegations in paragraphs 1–7 as if fully alleged herein.
9. Mr. Gordon denies the allegations of paragraph 9 and demands strict proof thereof.
10. Mr. Gordon denies the allegations of paragraph 10 and demands strict proof thereof.
11. Mr. Gordon denies the allegations of paragraph 11 and demands strict proof thereof.
12. The allegations in paragraph 12 are legal conclusions to which no response is required. To the extent a response is required, Oliver denies the allegations in paragraph 12 and demands strict proof thereof.

Mr. Gordon hereby denies any and all allegations in the Complaint not expressly admitted above.[2]

WHEREFORE, Mr. Gordon respectfully requests that the Court dismiss the Complaint with prejudice, award his costs and attorney's fees, and for such other and further relief as this Court deems just.[3]

---

[2] Although not required, it is standard practice to include a general denial, even when the defendant specifically addresses each paragraph.

[3] An answer must demand judgment and request relief.

AFFIRMATIVE DEFENSES

Pursuant to Fed. R. Civ. P. 8(c) [and local rule, if applicable], defendant Mr. Gordon asserts the following affirmative defenses:

FIRST AFFIRMATIVE DEFENSE

Ms. Kensington's claim is barred by accord and satisfaction.

SECOND AFFIRMATIVE DEFENSE

Ms. Kensington's claim is barred by release.

THIRD AFFIRMATIVE DEFENSE

Ms. Kensington's claim is barred by failure of consideration.

FOURTH AFFIRMATIVE DEFENSE

Ms. Kensington's claim is barred by the statute of fraud.

WHEREFORE, Mr. Gordon respectfully requests that the Court dismiss the Complaint with prejudice, award his costs and attorney's fees, and such other and further relief as this Court deems just.[4]

Dated[5]

---

[4] An answer must demand judgment and request relief on its affirmative defenses.

[5] The rules of the court in which the answer is filed determine who may sign it. In general, only an attorney admitted to practice in a particular court may sign documents filed in that court. Further, even if authorized by the court's rules to sign pleadings, junior associates should not presume that they will be signing them. It is advisable to check with the assigning attorney before signing any document to be filed with the court.

Sample Plaintiff's Proof Plan

PROOF PLAN: SECURITIES FRAUD

Elements	*Evidence*	*Issues*
• Misstatement press or omission regarding	• Defendant issues releases • Press releases overstated revenue and understated losses • After plaintiff purchased securities in defendant, defendant restated revenue and losses	
• In connection w/the purchase or sale of securities	• Plaintiff purchased securities in the defendant after issuance of the press releases	
• Misstatement/omission • Misstatement relates to a material fact • Plaintiff justifiably relied on defendant's statements/conduct	• Revenue and losses • Plaintiff relied on the defendants' press releases in making the decision to purchase the securities	• Nature of the losses[1] • Other information was available to the plaintiff
• Scienter	• Profit motive for officers and directors who held large portion of the securities in the defendant	• Did officers/directors actually profit? • What was the company's general practice with press releases? Was that practice followed?
• Defendant's conduct was the proximate cause of the injury to the plaintiff	• Defendant should have known of the true financial results	• Reasons for plaintiff's investment[2]

---

[1] Press release as opposed to restated numbers.
[2] When did D's and O's know that numbers in press release were wrong? Before or after?

Sample Plaintiff's Discovery Plan

DISCOVERY PLAN: SECURITIES FRAUD

Elements	Evidence	Discovery Method
• Misstatement or omission in connection with the purchase or sale of securities	• Press releases • Drafts of press releases • Restatements • Drafts of restatements • News reports • Statement/omission	• Document requests • Interrogatory identifying accountants, lawyers, etc.; subpoena duces tecum • Public sources of information, news reports, etc. • Document request: press release, financial statements, internal memos re: financial condition
	• Plaintiff's purchase	• Document requests to defendant • Obtain documents from plaintiff's broker
• Misstatement/omission of a material fact	• Revenue and losses • Statement/omission	• Legal argument • Document request: press release, financial statements, internal memos re: financial condition

EXHIBIT E—CONTINUED

Sample Plaintiff's Discovery Plan

DISCOVERY PLAN: SECURITIES FRAUD

Elements	Evidence	Discovery Method
• Plaintiff justifiably relied on defendant's statements/conduct	• Plaintiff relied on the defendant's press releases in making the decisions to purchase the securities • Purchase order	• Legal argument • Testimony of plaintiff • Document request: documentation of purchase
• Scienter	• Profit motive for officers and directors who sold large portion of the securities in the defendant • Defendant should have known of the true financial results	• Depose officers • Interrogatories and documents request related to personal profit • Document requests profit • Document requests • C Interrogatories regarding procedures
• Defendant's conduct was the proximate cause of the injury to the plaintiff		• Legal argument • Plaintiff's testimony

EXHIBIT F

Sample Certificate of Service

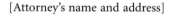

CERTIFICATE OF SERVICE

I hereby certify that on [date], copies of the foregoing [names of all documents to be served; include any attached affidavits/declarations, memoranda, and proposed orders] were served upon the following by [method—first-class U.S. Mail, postage, Federal Express, etc.; review your local rules and any relevant court orders for permissible means of delivery] pre-paid:

[Attorney's name and address]

[Attorney's name and address]

Angie Associate

Sample Interrogatories

UNITED STATES DISTRICT COURT FOR

THE SOUTHERN DISTRICT OF SURVIVAL[1]

INTERNATIONAL SIGNS, INC,)	
)	
Plaintiff,)	
v.)	Case No. 02-0001
RUBEY CORP.,)	
)	
Defendant.)	
)	

DEFENDANT'S FIRST SET OF INTERROGATORIES
TO PLAINTIFF[2]

Pursuant to Fed. R. Civ. P. 33 [and local rule, if applicable], defendant Rubey Corporation hereby propounds the following interrogatories to the plaintiff International Signs, Inc.

---

[1] The heading of discovery requests must provide the name of the court, the parties, and title of the action (e.g., A, plaintiff v. D, defendant), the case number and the nature of the pleading (e.g., interrogatories). The format and style of captions vary across jurisdictions. You should, therefore, review the requirements of the court's local rules and the common practice in that jurisdiction.

[2] The title of the discovery requests should identify who the requests are to, who the requests are from, the type of discovery requests, and the number of the requests (e.g., First, Second, etc.), if applicable.

Instructions and Definitions[3]

1. "Identify," when used with regard to a natural person, means to state the person's name, last known home address, last known home telephone number, last known work address, and last known work telephone number.
2. "Identify," when used with regard to an entity other than a natural person, means to state the entity's name, last known address, and last known telephone number and to describe the entity by type (e.g., a corporation).
3. "Identify," when used with regard to a document, shall mean to state the date and author, the persons to whom it was directed, the type of document (e.g., letter, memorandum, telegram, chart, etc.), its present location, including the location of each copy thereof, and the identity of its custodian. If any such document was but is no longer in your possession or subject to your control, state what disposition was made of it.
4. "Identify," when used with regard to a communication (as defined below), shall mean to state the date of the communication; whether the communication was written, oral, or electronic; and to identify all persons party to the communication.
5. "Document," when used herein, includes every tangible thing from which information can be obtained, perceived, reproduced, or communicated, either directly or with the aid of a machine or device, including, but not limited to, any handwritten, typed, printed, or graphic materials; any drawing, diagram, or chart; any photograph, slide, movie, videotape, or film; any recording, tape, disk, drum, or cassette; any computer data, punch data, or other data compilation, however stored or recorded; and all copies of any of the foregoing by whatever means made.
6. "Communication," when used herein, means the act or fact of communicating, whether orally, nonverbally, telephonically, electronically, telegraphically, in writing, by recording, or otherwise.
7. "You" and "Your," when used herein, means the plaintiff, International Signs, Inc., as defined below.
8. "International Signs," when used herein, means the plaintiff, International Signs, Inc., its agents, employees, representatives, accountants and attorneys, its parents, affiliates, divisions, controlled companies, subsidiaries and other related entities, the agents, employees, representatives, accountants and attorneys of those entities, and all other persons or entities, acting, or purporting to act, on its behalf.
9. "Rubey," when used herein, means the defendant, Rubey Corp., its agents, employees, representatives, accountants and attorneys, its parents, affiliates, divisions, controlled companies, subsidiaries and other related entities, the agents, employees, representatives, accountants, and attorneys of those entities, and all other persons or entities acting, or purporting to act, on its behalf.

---

[3] In the "Instructions and Definitions" section you may define terms used in the discovery requests, and provide instructions on the manner in which you wish the adverse party to respond to your requests. Note, however, that to the extent the instructions and definitions provided exceed the scope of permissible discovery, they may be objectionable. Also, refer to your local rules to determine if the court has mandatory or permissive instructions and definitions.

10. The "January 23 Memorandum," when used herein, means the January 23 Memorandum You alleged to exist in paragraph 4 of Your complaint.

11. In answering these interrogatories, all language shall be given its plain meaning.

12. Whenever a date, amount, or other computation or figure is requested in these interrogatories, the exact date, amount, or other computation or figure is required if known. If only approximate dates, amounts, or other computations or figures are known, then those approximations shall be given and stated as such, to the best of Your knowledge or belief.

13. If an answer to an interrogatory is not known, then that lack of knowledge must be specifically indicated in the response. If any information requested is not in Your possession but is known or believed to be in the possession of another person, identify that person and state the basis for Your belief or knowledge that the requested information is in that person's possession.

14. When an interrogatory does not specifically request a fact, but the additional fact is necessary to make the interrogatory response comprehensible, complete, or not misleading, the interrogatory should be deemed to include a specific request for that fact.

15. If You consider any requested information to be privileged or otherwise exempt from discovery, then provide a privilege log of such information withheld, identifying the content sufficient to ascertain whether or not the information is privileged or otherwise exempt in whole or part.

16. These interrogatories are continuing in nature, requiring that Your answers be amended or supplemented in the event that different or additional information becomes available to You or Your agents, employees, representatives, accountants, or attorneys.

Interrogatories[4]

1. Identify all persons whom you believe have personal knowledge of facts supporting the allegations set forth in Your complaint and, for each such person, describe the nature of the matters concerning which such person has knowledge.[5]

2. Identify each person whom You expect to call as an expert witness at or in connection with the hearing in this case, together with the subject matter on which the expert is expected to testify, the substance of the facts and opinions to which the expert is expected to testify, and a summary of the grounds for each opinion; and identify each document or communication that serves as the basis for, that supports, or that otherwise discusses, refers to, or relates in any way to Your response.

3. Identify each person whom you expect to call as a fact witness at or in connection with the hearing in this case, together with the subject matter on which the witness is expected to testify.

---

[4] This section states each interrogatory separately.

[5] This is an example of an information-seeking interrogatory. If the court in which the case is pending has adopted Fed. R. Civ. P. 26(a)(1), this request may not be necessary because it duplicates information required in the Initial Disclosures.

4. Identify each witness statement taken by or on behalf of International Signs in connection with the claims made in the complaint, whether such statement was transcribed, video recorded, tape recorded, or otherwise preserved in any way, including in Your response the name of the witness or witnesses, the date of the statement, and the identities of all others present during the taking of the statement.

5. Describe in detail all communications with anyone that refer or relate to the subject matter of the complaint, and identify all documents that comprise, refer, or relate to any such communications.

6. Identify all facts that support the allegation in paragraph 4 of Your complaint that "there existed a valid, binding, and enforceable contract between International Signs and Rubey."[6]

7. Identify the type and location of work You allege that the January 23 Memorandum requires Rubey to perform.

8. Identify the consideration exchanged under the January 23 Memorandum.

9. Identify all facts that support the allegation in paragraph 9 of Your complaint that Rubey breached the January 23 Memorandum.

10. Describe in detail all steps taken to mitigate Your damages in this action.

11. Describe in detail how You calculate the damages that You are requesting in this action.

Dated[7]
    [Name of attorney(s) of record]
    [Bar No., if required]
    [Firm]
    [Address]
    [Phone and fax numbers]

---

[6] This is an example of a contention interrogatory.

[7] Even though discovery requests generally are not filed in court, the rules of the court in which the case is pending regarding who is eligible to sign pleadings still apply. Junior associates should not presume that they will be signing discovery requests to the adverse parties and should, instead, check with the assigning attorney before signing any document.

Sample Requests for Production

UNITED STATES DISTRICT COURT FOR

THE SOUTHERN DISTRICT OF SURVIVAL[1]

INTERNATIONAL SIGNS, INC,)	
)	
Plaintiff,)	
v.)	Case No. 02-0001
RUBEY CORP.,)	
)	
Defendant.)	
)	

DEFENDANT'S FIRST REQUESTS FOR
PRODUCTION TO PLAINTIFF[2]

Pursuant to Fed. R. Civ. P. 34 and [and local rule, if applicable], defendant Rubey Corporation hereby propounds the following interrogatories to the plaintiff International Signs, Inc.

---

[1] The heading of discovery requests must provide the name of the court, the parties and title of the action (e.g., A, plaintiff v. D, defendant), the case number and the nature of the pleading (e.g., Complaint). The format and style of captions vary across jurisdictions. You should, therefore, review the requirements of the court's local rules and the common practice in that jurisdiction.

[2] The title of the discovery requests should identify who the requests are to, who the requests are from, the type of discovery requests, and the number of the requests (e.g., First, Second, etc.), if applicable.

Instructions and Definitions[3]

1. "Document," when used herein, includes every tangible thing from which information can be obtained, perceived, reproduced, or communicated, either directly or with the aid of a machine or device, including, but not limited to, any handwritten, typed, printed, electronic, or graphic materials; any drawing, diagram, or chart; any photograph, slide, movie, videotape, or film; any recording, tape, disk, drum, or cassette; any computer data, punch data, or other data compilation, however stored or recorded; and all copies of any of the foregoing by whatever means made.

2. "Communication," when used herein, means the act or fact of communicating, whether orally, nonverbally, telephonically, telegraphically, electronically, in writing, by recording, or otherwise.

3. "Concerning," when used herein, means evidencing, supporting, contradicting, constituting, referring, or otherwise relating to.

4. "You" and "Your," when used herein, means the plaintiff, International Signs, Inc., as defined below.

5. "International Signs," when used herein, means the plaintiff, International Signs, Inc., its agents, employees, representatives, accountants and attorneys, its parents, affiliates, divisions, controlled companies, subsidiaries and other related entities, the agents, employees, representatives, accountants, and attorneys of those entities, and all other persons or entities acting, or purporting to act, on its behalf.

6. "Rubey," when used herein, means the defendant, Rubey Corporation, its agents, employees, representatives, accountants and attorneys, its parents, affiliates, divisions, controlled companies, subsidiaries and other related entities, the agents, employees, representatives, accountants, and attorneys of those entities, and all other persons or entities acting, or purporting to act, on its behalf.

7. The "January 23 Memorandum," when used herein, means the January 23 Memorandum You alleged to exist in paragraph 4 of your complaint.

8. This request for production of documents covers all documents in your possession, custody, or control as well as the possession, custody, or control of Your agents, employees, representatives, accountants, and attorneys.

9. This request for production of documents is continuing in nature, requiring that Your response be supplemented and additional documents be made available for inspection and copying in the event that additional documents covered by the request come into Your possession, custody, or control or the possession, custody, or control of Your agents, employees, representatives, accountants, and attorneys.

10. When two or more otherwise identical copies of a document bear different notations, underlinings, or other markings, each such copy should be produced.

---

[3] In the "Instructions and Definitions" section you may define terms used in the discovery requests, and provide instructions on the manner in which you wish the adverse party to respond to your requests. Note, however, that to the extent the instructions and definitions provided exceed the scope of permissible discovery, they may be objectionable. Also, refer to your local rules to determine if the court has mandatory or permissive instructions and definitions.

11. If any document requested herein was in Your possession, custody, or control, but has since been disposed of, lost, discarded, or destroyed or is otherwise unavailable, please provide the following for each such document:
    a. The nature or type of the document including any title or identifying number thereon;
    b. The date of its origin or preparation;
    c. The name of its author or originator;
    d. The name of its addressee, if any;
    e. The name of all recipients of any copy of the document;
    f. A summary of its substance;
    g. The time period during which the document was in Your possession, custody, or control;
    h. The name and address of any person or entity who, to the best of Your knowledge, has a copy of the document;
    i. The date of the disposition, loss, discarding, or destruction of the document, or the date when the document became unavailable; and
    j. The reason for the disposition, loss, discarding, destruction, or unavailability of the document and the identity of the person, if any, responsible therefore.
12. File folders with tabs or labels identifying documents responsive to this request should be produced intact with such documents.
13. Documents attached to each other should not be separated.
14. If responsive documents are kept together in the usual course of business, they should be so produced, in order to fairly reveal and not to distort the nature of Your filing and record keeping system.
15. Electronic records and computerized information should be produced:
    a. in an intelligible format; or
    b. together with a description of the system from which they were obtained sufficient to render the records and information intelligible.
16. When there are no documents in Your possession, custody, or control, which are responsive to a particular category in this request, please so state.
17. If You object to the production of any document on the basis of some privilege, provide a schedule that lists each document withheld, a general description of that document (including its date, its author, each recipient, and the type of document), a statement of the privilege asserted and the basis for the assertion of that privilege.
18. Unless a different time period is specified, the applicable time period for each document request is December 1, 2000, to the present.

Documents Requested[4]

1. All documents concerning the January 23 Memorandum.
2. All documents concerning the facts and claims alleged in Your complaint.
3. All documents comprising or relating to communications with any representative of Rubey concerning the subject matter of this action.

---

[4] State each document request separately.

4. All documents that You have provided to any person(s) whom You expect to call as an expert witness at the hearing, as well as all documents that the person(s) whom You expect to call as an expert witness at trial has reviewed, created, or adopted in any way in connection with this action. This request includes, but is not limited to, the following:

   a. All written reports of each person whom You expect to call as an expert witness as trial;

   b. The most recent resume of or curriculum vitae of each person whom You expect to call as an expert witness at trial;

   c. All notes, diagrams, photographs, or other documents prepared or reviewed in connection with their assignment in this case by each person whom You intend to call as an expert witness at trial;

   d. For each person whom You intend to call as an expert witness at trial, all drafts, working papers, or documents generated by that person in connection with the opinions and subjects on which that person is expected to testify;

   e. Each publication or paper that was written or worked on by each witness whom You intend to call as an expert at trial, or which refers or relates to the opinions and subjects on which the witness is expected to testify; and

   f. Every transcript of prior deposition or trial testimony given by each person whom You intend to call as an expert witness at trial.

5. All written or recorded statements of Rubey concerning the subject matter of this action.

6. All documents concerning the communications with a representative of Rubey that are alleged in paragraphs 3 and 4 of Your complaint.

7. All documents identified in response to, or which form the basis of Your response to, Rubey's interrogatories to You.

8. All documents concerning any attempt by You to mitigate Your damages in this action.

9. All documents concerning the damages You claim in this action.

Dated[5]
    [Name of attorney(s) of record]
    [Bar No., if required]
    [Firm]
    [Address]
    [Phone and fax numbers]

---

[5] A sample Notice of Deposition is attached as Exhibit J.

EXHIBIT I

Sample Request for Admission

UNITED STATES DISTRICT COURT FOR

THE SOUTHERN DISTRICT OF SURVIVAL[1]

ROCKFORD HENRY,	)	
	)	
Plaintiff,	)	
v.	)	Case No. 02-0001
ABIGAIL HARRISON,	)	
	)	
Defendant.	)	
	)	

PLAINTIFF'S FIRST REQUEST FOR ADMISSIONS TO DEFENDANT[2]

Pursuant to Fed. R. Civ. P. 36 [and local rule, if applicable], plaintiff Rockford Henry, through counsel, respectfully requests that defendant Abigail Harrison admit the following matters for purposes of this action. If You fail to respond to this Request for Admissions in writing within 30 days of service of this Request, each matter set forth in this request will be deemed admitted and conclusively established against You for purposes of this action.

---

[1] The heading of discovery requests must provide the name of the court, the parties and title of the action (e.g., A, plaintiff v. D, defendant), the case number and the nature of the pleading (e.g., requests for admissions). The format and style of captions vary across jurisdictions. You should, therefore, review the requirements of the court's local rules and the common practice in that jurisdiction.

[2] The title of the discovery requests should identify who the requests are to, who the requests are from, the type of discovery requests, and the number of requests.

REQUESTS

ADMIT THAT:

Request No. 1: On July 2, 1999, Mr. Henry and Ms. Harrison entered into an agreement for personal services.

Request No. 2: The document attached hereto as Exhibit 1 is a true and correct copy of the July 2, 1999, agreement for personal services between Mr. Henry and Ms. Harrison.

Dated[3]
    [Name of attorney(s) of record]
    [Bar No., if required]
    [Firm]
    [Address]
    [Phone and fax numbers]

---

[3] Even though discovery requests generally are not filed in court, the rules of the court in which the case is pending regarding who is eligible to sign pleadings still apply. Junior associates should not presume that they will be signing discovery requests to the adverse parties and should, instead, check with the assigning attorney before signing any document.

Sample Notice of Deposition

UNITED STATES DISTRICT COURT FOR

THE SOUTHERN DISTRICT OF SURVIVAL[1]

MADDIE JOHNSON,	)	
	)	
Plaintiff,	)	
v.	)	Case No. 02-0001
P. PARR,	)	
	)	
Defendant.	)	
	)	

DEFENDANT P. PARR'S NOTICE OF DEPOSITION[2]

PLEASE TAKE NOTICE THAT, pursuant to Fed. R. Civ. Pro. 26 and 30 [and local rule, if applicable], the deposition upon oral examination[3] of plaintiff Maddie Johnson[4] will be taken by defendant P. Parr,[5] through its undersigned counsel, on March 9, 2001 at 10:00 a.m.[6] at the offices of Zachary and Associates, LLP, 123 First Street, Macon, GA, 31207,[7] before an officer authorized by law to administer

---

[1] The heading of a deposition notice must provide the name of the court, the parties and title of the action (e.g., A, plaintiff v. D, defendant), the case number and the nature of the pleading (e.g., Notice of Deposition). The format and style of captions vary across jurisdictions. You should, therefore, review the requirements of the court's local rules and the common practice in that jurisdiction.

[2] The title of the deposition notice should identify who is noticing the deposition and the name of the person whose deposition is noticed.

[3] Identify the type of deposition.

[4] Identify who will be deposed.

[5] Identify the party who is taking the deposition.

[6] Identify the date and time of the deposition.

[7] Identify the location of the deposition.

oaths.[8] The deposition shall continue from day to day until completed, excluding weekends and holidays,[9] and shall be recorded stenographically.[10] This deposition is taken both for purposes of discovery and for the use as evidence at trial.[11]

Dated[12]
    [Name of attorney(s) of record]
    [Bar No., if required]
    [Firm]
    [Address]
    [Phone and fax numbers]

---

[8] Indicate that the deposition will be under oath.

[9] State that the deposition will continue until it is completed. This will protect you by providing the presumptive right to continue the deposition to the next day if you were not permitted to depose the witness for the seven hours permitted under the Federal Rules.

[10] Indicate the method by which the deposition will be recorded.

[11] Indicate the purpose of the deposition.

[12] Even though deposition notices generally are not filed in court, the rules of the court in which the case is pending regarding who is eligible to sign pleadings still apply. Junior associates should not presume that they will be signing deposition notices and should, instead, check with the assigning attorney before signing any document.

Sample Motion to Dismiss under Rule 12(b)(6)

UNITED STATES DISTRICT COURT FOR

THE SOUTHERN DISTRICT OF SURVIVAL[1]

ANNABELLE,	)	
	)	
Plaintiff,	)	
v.	)	Case No. 02-0001
HARLEY,	)	
	)	
Defendant.	)	
	)	

MOTION TO DISMISS[2]

Harley, through counsel and pursuant to FED. R. CIV. P. 12(b)(6) [and local rule, if applicable], respectfully submits this Motion to Dismiss plaintiff Annabelle's complaint. Annabelle's complaint alleges one cause of action against Harley for breach of contract. Under the bare allegations of the complaint, however, it is evident that Annabelle failed to file her alleged breach of contract claim against Harley before the expiration of the applicable statute of limitation for such a claim. See WHWT Code

---

[1] The heading of discovery requests must provide the name of the court, the parties and title of the action (e.g., A, plaintiff v. D, defendant), the case number and the nature of the pleading (e.g., requests for admissions). The format and style of captions vary across jurisdictions. You should, therefore, review the requirements of the court's local rules and the common practice in that jurisdiction.

[2] The title of the motion should identify the moving party.

Ann. § 9-14. Thus, even if true, the allegations of the complaint establish that Annabelle's claim against Harley is time-barred. Accordingly, Annabelle has failed to state a claim on which relief may be granted and her complaint must be dismissed.

A memorandum of points and authorities accompanies this motion.

      Respectfully submitted,

Dated[3]
    [Name of attorney(s) of record]
    [Bar No., if required]
    [Firm]
    [Address]
    [Phone and fax numbers]

---

[3] The rules of the court in which the motion is filed determine who may sign it. In general, only an attorney admitted to practice in a particular court may sign documents filed in that court. Further, even if authorized by the court's rules to sign pleading, junior associates should not presume that they will be signing them. It is advisable to check with the assigning attorney before signing any document to be filed with the court.

Sample Memorandum of Points and Authorities

UNITED STATES DISTRICT COURT FOR

THE SOUTHERN DISTRICT OF SURVIVAL[1]

ANNABELLE,	)	
	)	
Plaintiff,	)	
v.	)	Case No. 02-0001
HARLEY,	)	
	)	
Defendant.	)	
	)	

MEMORANDUM OF POINTS AND AUTHORITIES
IN SUPPORT OF OLIVER'S MOTION TO DISMISS[2]

Harley, through counsel and pursuant to FED. R. CIV. P. 12(b)(6) [and local rule, if applicable], respectfully submits this memorandum of points and authorities in support of his Motion to Dismiss the plaintiff Annabelle's complaint against him.

---

[1] The heading of a memorandum must provide the name of the court, the parties and title of the action (e.g., A, plaintiff v. D, defendant), the case number and the nature of the pleading (e.g., memorandum in support of Motion to Dismiss). Fed. R. Civ. P. 10(a). The format and style of captions vary across jurisdictions. You should, therefore, review the requirements of the court's local rules and the common practice in that jurisdiction.

[2] The title of the memorandum should identify the moving party.

BACKGROUND [OR STATEMENT OF FACTS]

[State the relevant allegations from the complaint and any documents attached thereto.]

ARGUMENT

[Under as many separate headings and subheadings as required, provide each point and legal argument that supports the motion. The headings and subheadings should provide the roadmap of Your argument and, when read alone, indicate the entire basis of the motion. Focus on the cases that constitute binding authority in the court in which the action is pending that have the "right" result.]

CONCLUSION

WHEREFORE, Harley respectfully requests that all claims of the plaintiff Annabelle's complaint be dismissed with prejudice for failure to state a claim upon which relief may be granted.

Respectfully submitted,

Dated[3]

    [Name of attorney(s) of record]
    [Bar No., if required]
    [Firm]
    [Address]
    [Phone and fax numbers]

---

[3] The rules of the court in which the memorandum is filed determine who may sign it. In general, only an attorney admitted to practice in a particular court may sign documents filed in that court. Further, even if authorized by the court's rules to sign pleading, junior associates should not presume that they will be signing them. It is advisable to check with the assigning attorney before signing any document to be filed with the court.

EXHIBIT L

Sample Statement of Undisputed Material Facts

UNITED STATES DISTRICT COURT FOR
THE SOUTHERN DISTRICT OF SURVIVAL[1]

OLIVIA KENSINGTON,	)	
	)	
Plaintiff,	)	
v.	)	Case No. 02-0001
OLIVER GORDON,	)	
	)	
Defendant.	)	
	)	

OLIVER'S STATEMENT OF UNDISPUTED MATERIAL FACTS[2]

Pursuant to [local rule], defendant Oliver, through counsel, submits the following material facts as to which there is no genuine issue and entitled defendant Oliver to judgment as a matter of law:

---

[1] The heading of a motion must provide the name of the court, the parties and title of the action (e.g., A, plaintiff v. D, defendant), the case number and the nature of the pleading (e.g., statement of material facts as to which there is no genuine dispute). Fed. R. Civ. P. 10(a). The format and style of captions vary across jurisdictions. You should, therefore, review the requirements of the court's local rules and the common practice in that jurisdiction.

[2] The title should identify who is making the statement.

1. [State each of the material, undisputed facts with citations to the record.] [need examples of facts, discussion of "citations to the record."]

Respectfully submitted,

Dated[3]
　　[Name of attorney(s) of record]
　　[Bar No., if required]
　　[Firm]
　　[Address]
　　[Phone and fax numbers]

---

[3] The rules of the court in which the statement is filed determine who may sign it. In general, only an attorney admitted to practice in a particular court may sign documents filed in that court. Further, even if authorized by the court's rules to sign pleading, junior associates should not presume that they will be signing them. It is advisable to check with the assigning attorney before signing any document to be filed with the court.

Sample Motion for Summary Judgment

UNITED STATES DISTRICT COURT FOR

THE SOUTHERN DISTRICT OF SURVIVAL[1]

OLIVIA KENSINGTON,	)	
	)	
Plaintiff,	)	
v.	)	Case No. 02-0001
OLIVER GORDON,	)	
	)	
Defendant.	)	
	)	

OLIVER GORDON'S MOTION FOR SUMMARY JUDGMENT[2]

Oliver Gordon, through counsel and pursuant to FED. R. CIV. P. 56 [and local rule, if applicable], respectfully submits this motion seeking summary judgment on plaintiff Olivia Kensington's complaint. Ms. Kensington's complaint alleges one cause of action against Mr. Gordon for fraudulent inducement to contract, in which she seeks to rescind that contract. After Ms. Kensington was on notice of Mr. Gordon's alleged fraud, however, Ms. Kensington affirmed the contract and is now barred from seeking

---

[1] The heading of a motion must provide the name of the court, the parties and title of the action (e.g., A, plaintiff v. D, defendant), the case number and the nature of the pleading (e.g., motion for summary judgment). Fed. R. Civ. P. 10(a). The format and style of captions vary across jurisdictions. You should, therefore, review the requirements of the court's local rules and the common practice in that jurisdiction.

[2] The title of the motion should identify the moving party and the party against whom the motion is made.

to rescind it. Accordingly, Mr. Gordon requests that Ms. Kensington's complaint against him be dismissed with prejudice.

A memorandum of points and authorities accompanies this motion.

Respectfully submitted,

Dated[3]

    [Name of attorney(s) of record]
    [Bar No., if required]
    [Firm]
    [Address]
    [Phone and fax numbers]

---

[3] The rules of the court in which the motion is filed determine who may sign it. In general, only an attorney admitted to practice in a particular court may sign documents filed in that court. Further, even if authorized by the court's rules to sign pleading, junior associates should not presume that they will be signing them. It is advisable to check with the assigning attorney before signing any document to be filed with the court.

Sample Memorandum of Points and Authorities

UNITED STATES DISTRICT COURT FOR

THE SOUTHERN DISTRICT OF SURVIVAL[1]

OLIVIA KENSINGTON,	)	
	)	
Plaintiff,	)	
v.	)	Case No. 02-0001
OLIVER GORDON,	)	
	)	
Defendant.	)	
	)	

**MEMORANDUM OF POINTS AND AUTHORITIES IN SUPPORT OF
OLIVER GORDON'S MOTION FOR SUMMARY JUDGMENT[2]**

Oliver Gordon, through counsel and pursuant to FED. R. CIV. P. 56 and L. CIV. R. 56.1, respectfully submits this memorandum of points and authorities in support of his motion for summary judgment on the plaintiff Olivia Kensington's complaint.

---

[1] The heading of a motion must provide the name of the court, the parties and title of the action (e.g., A, plaintiff v. D, defendant), the case number and the nature of the pleading (e.g., memorandum in support of motion for summary judgment). Fed. R. Civ. P. 10(a). The format and style of captions vary across jurisdictions. You should, therefore, review the requirements of the court's local rules and the common practice in that jurisdiction.

[2] The title of the memorandum should identify the moving party.

BACKGROUND

[Summarize the undisputed facts in narrative form, with citations to the Statement of Undisputed Facts.]

ARGUMENT

[Provide the legal standard for summary judgment. Analyze why summary judgment is appropriate under applicable case law, weaving in a discussion of the undisputed facts.]

CONCLUSION

WHEREFORE [or, alternatively, FOR THE FOREGOING REASONS], defendant Oliver respectfully requests that all claims in Olivia's complaint be dismissed against Oliver with prejudice.

Respectfully submitted,

Dated[3]

    [Name of attorney(s) of record]
    [Bar No., if required]
    [Firm]
    [Address]
    [Phone and fax numbers]

---

[3] The rules of the court in which the memorandum is filed determine who may sign it. In general, only an attorney admitted to practice in a particular court may sign documents filed in that court. Further, even if authorized by the court's rules to sign pleading, junior associates should not presume that they will be signing them. It is advisable to check with the assigning attorney before signing any document to be filed with the court.

Sample Motion to Compel Discovery

UNITED STATES DISTRICT COURT FOR

THE SOUTHERN DISTRICT OF SURVIVAL[1]

HOLEY PANTS CORP.,	)	
	)	
Plaintiff,	)	
v.	)	Case No. 02-0001
SLOBS, INC.,	)	
	)	
Defendant.	)	
	)	

SLOBS INC.'S MOTION TO COMPEL HOLEY PANTS, CORP. TO RESPOND ADEQUATELY TO PERDUE'S FIRST SET OF INTERROGATORIES[2]

Defendant Slobs, Inc. ("Slobs"), through counsel and pursuant to Fed. R. Civ. P. 37 [and local rule, if applicable], hereby moves to compel adequate responses from plaintiff Holey Pants, Corp. ("Holey Pants") to Slobs's first set of interrogatories to Holey Pants. Slobs also requests that this Court require Holey Pants pay the reasonable costs, including attorneys fees, incurred in making this motion pursuant to

---

[1] The heading of a motion must provide the name of the court, the parties and title of the action (e.g., A, plaintiff v. D, defendant), the case number and the nature of the pleading (e.g., motion to compel). Fed. R. Civ. P. 10(a). The format and style of captions vary across jurisdictions. You should, therefore, review the requirements of the court's local rules and the common practice in that jurisdiction.

[2] The title of the motion should identify the moving party and the party against whom the motion is made.

Fed. R. Civ. P. 37(a)(4)(A) [and local rule, if applicable]. The grounds for this motion are set forth in the accompanying memorandum.

Pursuant to Fed. R. Civ. P. 37(a)(2) [and local rule, if applicable] counsel for Slobs attempted to confer in good faith with counsel for Holey Pants in an effort to obtain the requested discovery without court intervention. The parties will be unable to reach an agreement.[3]

> Respectfully submitted,

Dated[4]
> [Name of attorney(s) of record]
> [Bar No., if required]
> [Firm]
> [Address]
> [Phone and fax numbers]

---

[3] Certify that you made an effort to resolve the discovery dispute without court intervention. In addition, in the memorandum in support of the motion you may want to describe your efforts and attach correspondence related

[4] The rules of the court in which the motion is filed determine who may sign it. In general, only an attorney admitted to practice in a particular court may sign documents filed in that court. Further, even if authorized by the court's rules to sign pleading, junior associates should not presume that they will be signing them. It is advisable to check with the assigning attorney before signing any document to be filed with the court.

Sample Memorandum of Points and Authorities

UNITED STATES DISTRICT COURT FOR

THE SOUTHERN DISTRICT OF SURVIVAL[1]

HOLEY PANTS CORP.,	)	
	)	
Plaintiff,	)	
v.	)	Case No. 02-0001
SLOBS, INC.,	)	
	)	
Defendant.	)	
	)	

MEMORANDUM OF POINTS AND AUTHORITIES IN SUPPORT OF SLOBS INC.'S MOTION TO COMPEL HOLEY PANTS, CORP. TO RESPOND ADEQUATELY TO SLOBS INC.'S FIRST SET OF INTERROGATORIES[2]

Defendant Slobs, Inc. ("Slobs"), through its attorneys, respectfully submits this memorandum of points and authorities in support of its motion to compel adequate

---

[1] The heading of a memorandum in support of a motion must provide the name of the court, the parties and title of the action (e.g., A, plaintiff v. D, defendant), the case number and the nature of the pleading (e.g., memorandum in support of a motion to compel). Fed. R. Civ. P. 10(a). The format and style of captions vary across jurisdictions. You should, therefore, review the requirements of the court's local rules and the common practice in that jurisdiction.

[2] The title of the memorandum should identify the moving party and the party against whom the motion is made.

responses from plaintiff Holey Pants Corp. ("Holey Pants") to the following interrogatory from Slobs's first set of interrogatories to Holey Pants.

BACKGROUND

[Provide a summary of the allegations to which the discovery request is relevant. Quote
in full the discovery request at issue and the adverse party's objections and/or response.
Attach correspondence related to Your efforts to resolve the discovery dispute. If the
opposing party has provided inadequate response, You should attach them.]

ARGUMENT

[Provide the legal standard for discovery and the type of discovery (interrogatories,
etc.) at issue. Analyze the reasons why the discovery sought is permissible and appropriate under applicable case law. Analyze the each of the responses and/or objections
provided by the adverse party under the applicable case law and explain how they are
inappropriate and/or inadequate. Analyze cases providing for the relief You request.]

CONCLUSION

For the foregoing reasons, defendant Slobs, Inc. [state the relief requested].

       Respectfully submitted,

Dated[3]

    [Name of attorney(s) of record]
    [Bar No., if required]
    [Firm]
    [Address]
    [Phone and fax numbers]

---

[3] The rules of the court in which the motion is filed determine who may sign it. In general, only an
attorney admitted to practice in a particular court may sign documents filed in that court. Further,
even if authorized by the court's rules to sign pleading, junior associates should not presume that they
will be signing them. It is advisable to check with the assigning attorney before signing any document
to be filed with the court.

Sample Settlement Agreement

CONFIDENTIAL SETTLEMENT AGREEMENT
AND MUTUAL GENERAL RELEASE

THIS CONFIDENTIAL SETTLEMENT AGREEMENT AND MUTUAL GENERAL RELEASE (the "Agreement") is made and entered into this 8th day of August, 1999, by Lady Enterprises and Buzzard's Rest, Inc. (the "Parties").[1]

I. DEFINITIONS

A. The term "Lawsuit" means the case captioned Lady Enterprises v. Buzzard's Rest, Inc., in the United States District Court for the District of Survival, Southern Division, Case No. 98-CV-0004.[2]

B. The term "Agreement" means the Supply Agreement between Lady Enterprises and Buzzard's Rest, Inc., dated June 1, 1996.

II. RECITALS

This Agreement between the Parties is for the purpose of settling any and all claims, controversies, or disputes between the Parties arising out of the Agreement that were raised, or could have been raised, in the Lawsuit. The Parties now wish to confidentially enter into this Agreement as a compromise of the claims of Lady Enterprises against Buzzard's Rest, Inc. without any admission of liability on the part of the Defendant.[3]

---

[1] This provision identifies the parties to the agreement.
[2] This provision identifies the litigation resolved by the agreement
[3] This provision states the purpose of the agreement.

III. GENERAL RELEASE[4]

A. Lady Enterprises, for and in consideration of the execution of this Mutual Release and payment of $325,000 (three hundred and twenty-five thousand dollars), and other good and valuable consideration receipt of which is hereby acknowledged, do hereby release, remise, and forever discharge the Buzzard's Rest, Inc. and its representatives, agents, assigns, dealers, affiliates, employees, officers, directors, successors, predecessors, parents, and subsidiaries, and all other persons or entities from any and all claims, debts, demands, rights and causes of action, damages, costs, expenses, and compensation of any nature whatsoever, whether based on tort, contract, or any other theory of recovery, and whether based on compensatory or punitive damages, by reason of any and all known or unknown, foreseen or unforeseen consequences, from the beginning of the world until the date of this release including, but not limited to, every right, claim, debt, or cause of action asserted, or that could have been asserted, in the Lawsuit.

B. Further, Buzzard's Rest, Inc. and its respective, agents, assigns, dealers, affiliates, employees, officers, directors, successors, predecessors, parents, and subsidiaries, by their respective counsel, hereby forever and fully release and discharge Lady Enterprises, its respective, agents, assigns, dealers, affiliates, employees, officers, directors, successors, predecessors, parents, and subsidiaries from all claims, demands, damages, actions, rights of action, liens, contribution, indemnity, and the like, which the undersigned now have or may hereafter have that arise out of or as a consequence of the Agreement. Buzzard's Rest, Inc., further agrees that this Confidential Settlement Agreement and Mutual General Release is in full accord and satisfaction of disputed claims and is not to be construed as an admission of any liability whatsoever by or on behalf of any signatory hereto, as by each of whom all liability is expressly denied.

IV. DISMISSAL OF ACTIONS[5]

Lady Enterprises, Inc. further agrees to dismiss the Lawsuit with prejudice, in accordance with the applicable rules of court, with the Parties to bear their own costs.

V. DISCLAIMER OF LIABILITY[6]

Lady Enterprises agrees and acknowledges that payment of the sum specified above, along with other consideration occasioned by the terms of this Agreement, serves as a full and complete compromise of all disputed issues as to Buzzard's Rest, Inc. related to the Agreement and/or raised in the Lawsuit; that neither payment of that sum by the Buzzard's Rest, Inc., nor the negotiations for this settlement (including all statements, admissions, or communications) by Buzzard's Rest, Inc. or its attorneys or representatives shall be considered admissions by the Buzzard's Rest, Inc. and same is hereby expressly denied by Buzzard's Rest, Inc., and that no past or present wrongdoing on the part of Buzzard's Rest, Inc. shall be implied by such payment or negotiations.

---

[4] This provision identifies the terms and scope of the mutual releases.
[5] This provision provides that the litigation will be dismissed with prejudice such that the litigation cannot be re-filed, and provides that each side bears its own costs.
[6] This provision provides all parties disclaim any liability on the claims asserted.

VI. NO OTHER CLAIMS[7]

Lady Enterprises warrants that it has the sole right and exclusive authority to make this Confidential Settlement Agreement and Mutual General Release, to give the release and to receive the sums specified, and it has not sold, assigned, transferred, conveyed, pledged, hypothecated, or otherwise disposed of or encumbered any of the claims or causes of action referred to in this Confidential Settlement Agreement and Mutual General Release. Buzzard's Rest, Inc. warrants that it has the sole right and exclusive authority to make this Confidential Settlement Agreement and Mutual General Release, to give the release and to receive the sums specified, and it has not sold, assigned, transferred, conveyed, pledged, hypothecated, or otherwise disposed of or encumbered any of the claims or causes of action referred to in this Confidential Settlement Agreement and Mutual General Release.

VII. ATTORNEYS' FEES AND COSTS[8]

The parties agree that all attorneys fees incurred Lady Enterprises as a result of the claims asserted in the Lawsuit, all existing or potential liens and subrogation claims, and all other costs and expenses incurred by or on behalf of Lady Enterprises in connection with the claims asserted in the Lawsuit and the settlement, shall be paid in full or satisfied from the settlement sum described in Section III.A. of this Confidential Settlement Agreement and Mutual General Release.

VIII. INTEGRATION[9]

This Confidential Settlement Agreement and Mutual General Release supersedes all prior agreements, negotiations, or understandings, whether written or oral, between the parties. No promise, agreement, statement, or representation not expressed herein has been made to, or been relied upon, by the parties and this document contains the entire agreement between the Parties.

IX. COMPLETE AND FINAL AGREEMENT[10]

Lady Enterprises agrees and acknowledges that it accepts the Agreement in full and complete settlement and as a final resolution of all disputed claims and issues against Buzzard's Rest, Inc. arising from the Agreement, or that were raised, or could have been raised, in the Lawsuit.

---

[7] This provision establishes that the parties have authority to provide the releases and give and receive the consideration therefore.

[8] This provision also provides that the releasing party bears no liability on any claims against the consideration for the release.

[9] This provision establishes that the settlement agreement and release is an integrated document, and that all promises or inducements for the settlement.

[10] This provision establishes that the claimant accepts the settlement and release in full satisfaction of all its claims.

X. CHOICE OF LAW[11]

The Agreement shall be deemed to be executed in the State of Texas and subject to and construed in accordance with the law of that state.

XI. SEVERABILITY[12]

If any part or provision of this Confidential Settlement Agreement and Mutual General Release should be held void or invalid, the remaining provisions shall remain in full force and effect.

XII. ADVICE OF COUNSEL[13]

The Parties each acknowledge that each has had this Confidential Settlement Agreement and Mutual General Release fully explained to it by counsel of its choice and that it understands the words and terms used and their effect. Lady Enterprises realizes that this is a full and final compromise, release, settlement, and resolution of all claims it has against the Buzzard's Rest, Inc. and that this Confidential Settlement Agreement and Mutual General Release is signed as its free act and deed.

XIII. CONFIDENTIALITY[14]

In further consideration of the agreements herein, the parties and their legal counsel agree that they will not disclose and will take reasonable steps to prevent disclosure of this settlement without first obtaining the written permission of Buzzard's Rest, Inc. This non-disclosure provision includes:

a. The amount of any settlement demand by Lady Enterprises or on it behalf;

b. The amount of any settlement offered by Buzzard's Rest, Inc.;

c. The exact or approximate amount of the agreed settlement; and,

d. Any qualitative description of the settlement or the amount of the settlement.[15]

Lady Enterprises understands that Buzzard's Rest, Inc. has required it to include the non-disclosure provision above as a condition of settlement. The parties understand and agree to submit to the exclusive jurisdiction of the United States District Court for the District of Survival for any remedies related to breach of the terms of this Agreement.

XIV. COUNTERPARTS[16]

This Agreement may be executed in counterparts, in which case, upon delivery, each such counterpart shall be sufficient against the party signing it.

---

[11] This provision chooses the law under which the settlement agreement and release will be interpreted.

[12] This provision provides, in the event one provision of the settlement agreement and release is held to be void, the rest of the agreement is still enforceable.

[13] This provision establishes that the parties consulted with counsel and understand the settlement agreement and release.

[14] This provision protects against disclosure of the agreement and its terms.

[15] This provision is a forum selection clause, which requires that any litigation arising out of the settlement agreement and release will be litigated in a certain forum.

[16] This provision establishes that the parties may execute separate copies of the settlement agreement and release.

Sample Notice of Dismissal

UNITED STATES DISTRICT COURT FOR

THE SOUTHERN DISTRICT OF SURVIVAL[1]

LADY ENTERPRISES,	)	
	)	
Plaintiff,	)	
v.	)	Case No. 02-0001
BUZZARD'S REST, INC,	)	
	)	
Defendant.	)	
	)	

STIPULATED DISMISSAL WITH PREJUDICE[2]

The parties, through counsel, stipulate to dismiss the above-captioned action with prejudice according to the terms of a mutual settlement agreement executed by both parties on June 17, 2003.[3]

---

[1] The heading of a stipulated dismissal must provide the name of the court, the parties, and title of the action (e.g., A, plaintiff v. D, defendant), the case number and the nature of the pleading. The format and style of captions vary across jurisdictions. You should, therefore, review the requirements of the court's local rules and the common practice in that jurisdiction.

[2] The title of the stipulated dismissal should identify whether it is with or without prejudice. If a dismissal is with prejudice, the claims cannot be re-filed; if it is without prejudice, the claims can be re-filed.

[3] If a settlement agreement is confidential, do not attach it the stipulation of dismissal because it will become part of the public record available to anyone who asks to review the docket at the courthouse. However, if a settlement agreement is not confidential, you can attach the settlement agreement to the stipulation and proposed order of dismissal so that it becomes part of the order entered by the court. Counsel of record for both parties should sign the stipulated dismissal.

DATED:

    For the plaintiff _____

    For the defendant _____ [4]

Form Proposed Stipulated Order of Dismissal

UNITED STATES DISTRICT COURT FOR
THE SOUTHERN DISTRICT OF SURVIVAL[5]

LADY ENTERPRISES,	)	
	)	
Plaintiff,	)	
v.	)	Case No. 02-0001
BUZZARD'S REST, INC,	)	
	)	
Defendant.	)	
	)	

ORDER[6]

The Court has reviewed the Stipulation with Prejudice, and the terms and conditions of the Settlement Agreement attached to this Order as Exhibit 1 and incorporated in the Order as if fully set forth herein. Good cause appearing, it is

    ORDERED that the matter is dismissed with prejudice; and it is further

    ORDERED that this dismissal is expressly conditioned on the terms and conditions of the Settlement Agreement attached to and incorporated in this Order; and it is further

    ORDERED that this Court retains jurisdiction of this matter for the purposes of taking any action needed to enforce the terms of the attached Settlement Agreement and it is further

    ORDERED that each party will bear its own costs, as provided in the Settlement Agreement.

    SO ORDERED.

DATED:

---

[4] Counsel of record for both parties should sign the stipulated dismissal.

[5] The heading of an order must provide the name of the court, the parties, and title of the action (e.g., A, plaintiff v. D, defendant), the case number and the nature of the pleading. The format and style of captions vary across jurisdictions. You should, therefore, review the requirements of the court's local rules and the common practice in that jurisdiction.

[6] The title of document to be entered by the court should identify itself as an order.

Index